Will China Save the Planet?

This book is dedicated to the memory of my beloved parents, Roy Paul Finamore and Marie Gorman Finamore

Barbara Finamore

Will China Save the Planet?

polity

First published in 2018 by Polity Press
Reprinted: 2018, 2019

Polity Press
65 Bridge Street
Cambridge CB2 1UR, UK

Polity Press
101 Station Landing
Suite 300
Medford, MA 02155, USA

ISBN-13: 978-1-5095-3263-6
ISBN-13: 978-1-5095-3264-3(pb)

A catalogue record for this book is available from the British Library.

Library of Congress Cataloging-in-Publication Data
Names: Finamore, Barbara, author.
Title: Will China save the planet? / Barbara Finamore.
Description: Cambridge, UK ; Medford, MA, USA : Polity, 2018. | Series:
  Environmental futures | Includes bibliographical references and index.
Identifiers: LCCN 2018021605 (print) | LCCN 2018037960 (ebook) | ISBN
  9781509532667 (Epub) | ISBN 9781509532636 (hardback) | ISBN 9781509532643
  (pbk.)
Subjects: LCSH: Environmental policy--China. | Clean energy--China. | Energy
  policy--Environmental aspects--China. | China--Environmental conditions.
Classification: LCC GE190.C6 (ebook) | LCC GE190.C6 F56 2018 (print) | DDC
  363.7/05610951--dc23
LC record available at https://lccn.loc.gov/2018021605

Typeset in 11 on 15 pt Sabon by
Servis Filmsetting Ltd, Stockport, Cheshire
Printed and bound in the United States by LSC Communications

For further information on Polity, visit our website: politybooks.com

Contents

Acknowledgments

I would first like to thank my editor at Polity Press, Louise Knight, who persuaded me to write this book, and my extraordinarily helpful assistant editor Nekane Tanaka Galdos.

I am deeply indebted to the Natural Resources Defense Council's leadership, particularly its president Rhea Suh, as well as Susan Casey-Lefkowitz and Jake Schmidt, all of whom gave me the time I needed; and to NRDC's members and supporters, who made this project possible. Bob Deans, Edwin Chen, and Jenny Powers provided essential guidance and support. But I could never have written this book without the inspiration of John Adams, Tom Cochran, and Jacob Scherr, who brought me to NRDC in 1981; of Frances Beinecke, who opened our Beijing office; and of everyone who has been a part of our dedicated China team for nearly a quarter of a century.

Acknowledgments

Many thanks to the colleagues who took time to review the manuscript and provide invaluable comments: Alvin Lin, Fang Jian, Han Chen, Freda Fung, Jingjing Qian, and Mona Yew. Lynne Curry and several anonymous reviewers provided crucial feedback.

Many other colleagues contributed key research or insights: Lauren Sidner, Yang Fuqiang, Wang Wanxing, Wang Yan, Wu Qi, Zhang Xiya, Hyoungmi Kim, Kevin Hsu, Brian Bartholomew, Noah Lerner, Collin Smith, Charlotte Steiner, and Winslow Robertson. I would also like to acknowledge the contributions of many other colleagues, including Irina Petrova, Lauren Gruber, Lisa Goffredi, Valerie Keane, Alex Liu, Apurva Muchhala, and Hiawatha Barno.

No words can express my profound gratitude to friends and family for their unstinting support, especially my children Rebecca, Patrick, and Michael Young; my daughter-in-law Megan Wolf Young; and my siblings Marie, Roy, and Michael Finamore. Most of all, I wish to thank my beloved husband of 35 years, Stephen Young, who first brought me to China in 1990.

Abbreviations

ACEF	All-China Environment Federation
BNEF	Bloomberg New Energy Finance
BRI	Belt and Road Initiative
BTH	Beijing/Tianjin/Hebei
CAFE	Corporate Average Fuel Economy
CERC	Clean Energy Research Center (US–China)
CO_2	carbon dioxide
DR	demand response
EPL	Environmental Protection Law
ESG	environmental, social, and governance
EV	electric vehicle
FCV	fuel cell vehicle
FIT	feed-in tariff
FON	Friends of Nature
GDP	gross domestic product
GEI	Global Environmental Institute

Abbreviations

GFSG	G20 Green Finance Study Group
GHG	greenhouse gas
GW	gigawatt
ICE	internal combustion engine
IEA	International Energy Agency
IPCC	Intergovernmental Panel on Climate Change
IPE	Institute of Public & Environmental Affairs
kWh	kilowatt hour
LEED	Leadership in Energy and Environmental Design
MEE	Ministry of Ecology and Environment
MFA	Ministry of Foreign Affairs
MW	megawatt
NDC	Nationally Determined Contribution
NDRC	National Development and Reform Commission
NEA	National Energy Administration
NEV	new energy vehicle
NGO	nongovernmental organization
NOx	nitrogen oxides
NRDC	Natural Resources Defense Council
NREL	National Renewable Energy Laboratory
PM 2.5	fine particulate matter with diameters of 2.5 micrometers and smaller

Abbreviations

PM 10	large particulate matter with diameters of 10 micrometers or smaller
PRD	Pearl River Delta
PV	photovoltaic
RMB	Renminbi
RPS	Renewable Portfolio Standards
SEPA	State Environmental Protection Administration
SO_2	sulfur dioxide
SPC	State Planning Commission
TW	terawatt
UHV	ultra-high voltage
WTO	World Trade Organization
YRD	Yangtze River Delta
ZEV	zero emission vehicle

Introduction: China – The New Climate Torchbearer?

Donald Trump famously called climate change a "hoax" perpetrated by the Chinese to make US manufacturing noncompetitive. But the evidence is staring us in the face: climate change is real and it is happening now. How else can we explain a 50-fold increase since 1980 in the number of places experiencing life-threatening or extreme heat; a surge in catastrophic hurricanes, flooding, and raging wildfires; North Pole temperatures that have soared 50 degrees Fahrenheit above normal; and an iceberg weighing one trillion tons breaking off Antarctica?

Every major scientific organization in the world agrees that the Earth's climate is warming to dangerous levels and that humans are to blame. According to the World Meteorological Organization, current concentrations of carbon dioxide (CO_2) in the atmosphere correspond to a climate last occurring roughly 4 million years ago – a time when melting ice sheets caused sea levels to rise 60 feet higher than they are today.[1] Unless we act quickly and forcefully to drive down greenhouse gas (GHG) emissions, we will soon reach a climate tipping point, where disastrous consequences will harm every aspect of our life on Earth.

China's own climate scientists warn that it will face more frequent extreme weather events, glacier retreats, sea level rise higher than the world average, flooding, droughts, and food insecurity. Globally, experts predict that climate change will push an estimated 100 million people back into poverty by 2030,[2] and cause an additional 250,000 premature deaths each year between 2030 and 2050 from malnutrition, malaria, diarrhea, and heat stress.[3] Rising sea levels may render more than 1,000 low-lying tropical islands "uninhabitable" by the middle of the century – or even earlier.[4] The US Department of Defense called the impacts of climate change "threat multipliers that will aggravate stressors abroad such as poverty, environmental degradation, political instability and social tensions – conditions that can enable terrorist activity and other forms of violence."[5]

In the landmark 2015 Paris Agreement, the world's first truly global climate deal, nearly 200 countries agreed that the threat of climate change is "urgent and potentially irreversible" and can only be addressed through deep reductions in global carbon emissions. The deal aims to keep the rise in global average temperature to well below 2 degrees Celsius above pre-industrial levels and, if possible, under 1.5 degrees. The participating countries resolved to peak global greenhouse gas emissions as soon as possible, with rapid reductions thereafter, and to achieve net zero GHG emissions in the second half of this century. The Paris Agreement sends a clear market signal that the global economy is transitioning away from dirty fossil fuels toward a low-carbon future powered by clean energy, creating the largest new market opportunity of the twenty-first century.

As a vitally important first step, every country signed up to the Agreement submitted a pledge detailing how it will cut its GHG emissions. When taken together, however, current pledges will deliver at most only one-third of what is needed to protect us from the worst impacts of climate change. To address the limitations of this bottom-up approach, the accord contains a mechanism designed to ensure that countries regularly strengthen their commitments over time. The Agreement also provides support for developing countries, including small island states and others that are most vulnerable, in their efforts to reach their climate goals. It also establishes a more robust transparency framework for reporting each country's progress, though many of the operating rules have been left to future negotiations.

The United States and China are by far the two largest emitters of GHGs. Together, they are responsible for over 40 percent of global CO_2 emissions, though China's per capita emissions are still less than half those of the United States. Despite longstanding tensions between the two countries on a broad range of issues, Presidents Barack Obama and Xi Jinping presided over a remarkable era of bilateral climate cooperation. This extraordinary partnership played a critical role in building momentum for the Paris Agreement and influencing the remarkable speed with which it entered into force. Both leaders recognized that accelerating the transition to a green, low-carbon, and climate-resilient economy is not only crucial to addressing one of the greatest threats facing humanity, but is also in each country's own self-interest.

Yet despite support for the Paris Agreement from the overwhelming majority of US businesses and citizens, President Donald Trump has turned the United States into a global climate pariah. He has announced plans to withdraw America from the Agreement in 2020, slashed funding for US climate programs, attempted to dismantle the US Clean Power Plan, and promoted dirty fossil fuel development on US lands and in US waters. Furthermore, Trump muzzled US climate scientists and purged references to climate change risks from government websites and the US National Security Strategy. In July 2017, Trump stood alone at the annual G20 summit as the other 19 world leaders reaffirmed their strong commitment to the Paris Agreement and declared it to be "irreversible." By abandoning the Paris Agreement, the United States has become the only country in the world to say "no" to the massive economic opportunities that accompany the transition to a clean energy future. Even Nicaragua and Syria, the only two original holdouts to the Agreement, have now signed on. Although Trump campaigned on a pledge to put "America First," his reckless move effectively puts America last.

Many have noted that with Trump's decision to pull out of the Paris Agreement, the United States is retreating from its global role in fighting climate change, while China is stepping forward. It was only a few years ago that China seemed the unlikeliest of climate action standard-bearers. After decades of rapid growth, the country held the distinction of being responsible for more than one-quarter of all global carbon emissions – more than the United States and the European Union combined. So mammoth was the nation's carbon footprint, in fact, that it was often cited by defenders of the fossil fuel status quo as a rationale for American inaction. *Why should we break our backs reducing our emissions,* people would ask, *when China is just going to keep on burning coal like crazy and warming the planet anyway?*

But the dramatic measures taken by China in recent years to cut emissions, reduce its reliance on coal, and invest in renewables have turned this line of thinking on its head. It now appears that China – while still leading the world in both coal consumption and carbon emissions – is also leading the way forward to the clean energy future. That said, it also faces major challenges that some believe may be insurmountable.

In the December 2009 Copenhagen climate negotiations, China took much of the blame for the failure of participants to reach a legally binding climate agreement. Yet just a few years after the Copenhagen summit, President Xi Jinping not only played a crucial role in the Paris climate deal, but later called the Paris Agreement a "milestone in the history of climate governance" that should not be derailed. In a major speech to the National People's Congress in fall 2017 to report on his first five years in office, Xi went even further, clearly asserting China's climate leadership: "We will get actively involved in global environmental governance and fulfill our emissions reductions ... Taking a driving seat in international cooperation to respond to climate change, China has become an important participant, contributor, and torchbearer in the global endeavor for ecological civilization."[6]

How did China get to this point? What brought about this evolution from climate change resister to a forceful advocate of global climate governance? Can it overcome the fundamental obstacles hindering its decarbonization efforts? As it greens its own economy, is China in danger of outsourcing its carbon emissions to other countries? How is this clean energy revolution being driven, and what role can other countries play? This book seeks to shed some light on those questions and outline the implications for the United States and the rest of the world of China's dynamic new engagement on this critical issue.

1

China's Climate Diplomacy

ǀ

I was in the room when it happened. Nearly three decades ago, as an environmental attorney living in Beijing, I witnessed China's emergence on the international climate stage. It happened in June 1991, at a conference in a crowded ballroom at the elegant Kunlun Hotel. Ministers from 40 developing countries were listening to Premier Li Peng deliver a keynote speech. He explained that he had invited them to Beijing to develop a joint strategy for developing countries to use in negotiating a climate change treaty at the United Nations Conference on Environment and Development, which was to be held the following year in Rio de Janeiro.

This was a watershed moment in China's climate diplomacy – the first time the country positioned itself as the leading voice of the developing world on climate change. The outcome of that conference, the 1991 Beijing Ministerial Declaration on Environment and Development (Beijing Declaration), contained a series of basic principles, many of which were adopted in the 1992 United Nations Framework Convention on Climate Change (Framework Convention).

Addressing climate change was not high on the list of China's priorities at the time. Instead, as the economy was booming, the government was focused on building new power plants as quickly as possible. The goal was to drive industrial production and bring electricity to a rapidly expanding population that by 1990 already exceeded 1.1 billion. Coal, plentiful and cheap, was the energy source of choice, not just for power plants, but also for direct combustion by heavy industry and for heating and cooking in people's homes.

Because of China's heavy dependence on coal, its CO_2 emissions had already begun to rise sharply. In 1991, China became the world's second largest CO_2 emitter after the United States, although its per capita emissions were less than one-tenth those of the United States. To the extent that government leaders were thinking about environmental issues, however, they were more concerned about the severe air and water pollution that was already plaguing the country.

Nonetheless, when the international community began to confront the reality of global climate change, China played an active role from the start, in large part so as to be seen as a responsible global player. Shortly after the establishment of the Intergovernmental Panel on Climate Change (IPCC) in 1988, China launched its own climate change research program involving 40 projects and 20 ministries.[1] It also formed an interagency National Coordinating Panel on Climate Change, which, among other things, developed a series of internal guidelines for China to use in the international climate negotiations.[2]

The guidelines were the result of internal jockeying among different government bureaucracies with competing priorities – a key feature of most Chinese policymaking. China's fledgling State Environmental Protection Administration (SEPA), the precursor to today's Ministry of Ecology and Environment (MEE), was concerned about the potential threat of climate change and was willing to consider actions to limit GHG emissions.[3] SEPA also believed that China had a responsibility to participate in the treaty negotiations because it was a major contributor to the problem.[4] The State Meteorological Administration and the State Science and Technology Commission (the precursor to the Ministry of Science and Technology), which were overseeing climate change research and developing response strategies, were sympathetic to this approach.[5]

However, the views of more powerful agencies prevailed. The Ministry of Foreign Affairs (MFA), concerned about protecting China's national sovereignty, opposed the idea of legally binding international climate commitments.[6] The MFA also sought to ensure that China was treated with respect as an equal partner in international affairs – a reaction to a history of mistreatment by other countries – and to bolster China's international image after a period of diplomatic isolation.[7]

The State Planning Commission (SPC), the precursor to the National Development and Reform Commission (NDRC), which manages the country's economy, wanted to safeguard China's national interest, which it defined as ensuring unconstrained economic development. The SPC therefore opposed any limits on energy consumption that might interfere with the country's economic growth.[8] The SPC also viewed the climate change negotiations as an opportunity to obtain financial assistance and advanced technology.[9]

The resulting climate negotiation guidelines strongly reflected China's top foreign policy and economic development priorities: safeguarding China's sovereignty, protecting its national interest, and enhancing its international image.[10] Key principles included the following positions:

- Developed countries should take the lead in halting human-induced climate change considering their greater historic, current, and cumulative emissions.
- Developing countries have a right to develop and should not be obligated to undertake measures that might hinder development.
- International cooperation should be based on the principle of sovereign equality of all countries.
- Environmental considerations should not be used as an excuse for interference in the internal affairs of developing countries.
- Developed countries should provide new and additional funding and technology on favorable terms to developing countries to assist with their efforts to address climate change.[11]

These fundamental principles, which were largely incorporated into the Beijing Declaration, have served as the foundation of China's climate diplomacy through decades of negotiations. During the negotiations on the Framework Convention, for example, China argued successfully that developed and developing countries should be treated differently in accordance with their "common but differentiated responsibilities and respective capabilities."[12] But along with the Group of 77, a coalition of developing nations, China strongly opposed any differentiation *among* developing countries based on their comparative stages of development or economic growth, especially the creation of a category of "more advanced developing countries."[13] The Chinese were concerned that this approach might single them out for greater obligations because of the country's rapidly growing economy and burgeoning CO_2 emissions. They blocked the inclusion of any legally binding measures or timetables in the Framework Convention, even for developed countries, and also opposed efforts by the United States and others to include strong requirements for countries to measure and report their emissions, arguing that these would infringe upon national sovereignty.[14]

The Kyoto Protocol, adopted in 1997 as a follow-up to the Framework Convention, set legally binding obligations on developed countries to reduce their GHG emissions. China and other developing countries, however, were not obligated to reduce emissions, only to establish national emission inventories, report on national programs, exchange information, and pursue sustainable development.

The unwillingness of China and other developing countries to accept binding emission reduction obligations in the Kyoto Protocol was a major source of friction between the United States and China for many years, especially as the latter's CO_2 emissions continued to grow. But China's annual, cumulative, and per capita CO_2 emissions at the time of the Kyoto Protocol were still much smaller than those of the United States. China, moreover, had real concerns about the country's continued poverty and its relative lack of capacity to monitor and reduce emissions.

China and the Copenhagen Accord

In December 2009, world leaders gathered in Copenhagen in the hopes of negotiating a fair, ambitious and binding climate agreement. Much had changed in China since the days of the Beijing Declaration. Following its 2001 entry into the World Trade Organization (WTO), China was experiencing one of the best decades in global economic history, quadrupling its gross domestic product

(GDP) and nearly quintupling its exports.[15] Energy use had doubled between 2000 and 2007 as the country raced to keep up with the pace of development, building on average one new coal-fired power plant a week to support its heavy industry and manufacturing facilities. In 2006, China overtook the United States as the world's largest carbon emitter, and by 2009 it had become a net coal importer and the world's largest energy consumer.

This headlong economic development came at an enormous price in terms of widespread environmental destruction, including accelerating outdoor and indoor air pollution, toxic water, and widespread soil contamination. Factories and power plants belched black coal smoke containing sulfur and ash that made breathing a hazard as far away as South Korea and Japan.[16] A 2000 World Health Organization study estimated that outdoor air pollution in China was associated with about 300,000 premature deaths a year.[17] In 2006, China published its first green GDP report, which found that pollution caused a loss of over $80 billion in 2004, equivalent to about 3 percent of that year's GDP.[18]

My organization, the Natural Resources Defense Council (NRDC – not to be confused with the Chinese government agency NDRC), was the first international nongovernment organization (NGO) to launch a clean energy program in China. We began in the mid-1990s by promoting energy efficiency as the cheapest, quickest solution for cleaning up China's environment while supporting its continued economic development. We explained how California had kept its energy use per capita nearly flat for 40 years while growing its economy, saving consumers $65 billion since the 1970s, and avoiding the need for an estimated 30 large power plants. But China's leaders were, at that time, more focused on building new coal power plants to increase the supply of electricity, and believed that meeting growing power demand with new coal plants was the only solution.

That changed in the summer of 2004, when severe power shortages, the worst in two decades, swept across the country. The government ordered 24 provinces and municipalities to slash their power consumption. The economic impacts were enormous, as factories were required to shut down or operate on alternate weeks. Our efforts to promote energy efficiency finally began to gain attention. Along with the China–US Energy Efficiency Alliance (another NGO that I co-founded; now called the China–US Energy Innovation Alliance), we helped Jiangsu Province, California's sister province, launch China's first large-scale utility-funded incentive program to assist factory managers and building owners to install efficient technologies. The success of this program helped to convince seven government ministries in 2010 to jointly issue regulations turning it into a national program.

By the time of the 2009 Copenhagen summit, China was also focusing increased attention on the country's vulnerability to the impacts of climate change. China's first National Assessment Report on Climate Change, completed in 2006, described how global warming would exacerbate the country's already severe water shortages, endanger coastal cities, threaten natural resources, and jeopardize food security. In 2007, China published its National Climate Change Program, the first of any developing country. The document integrated much of the work the country was already doing into a comprehensive set of climate-related targets and timetables.

China's concerns about climate change gave it a stake in reaching a global agreement, rather than just protecting its own foreign policy and economic interests.[19] Yet to both China's leaders and the public, these dire climate scenarios still seemed distant compared to more immediate concerns. As a result, China's international climate negotiations continued to operate largely on a separate track from the country's domestic climate policies. Negotiators continued to believe that the country's primary national interest was in protecting its unfettered economic growth. They remained intent on avoiding binding international commitments that might impede that growth or threaten China's national sovereignty.

Nevertheless, China did make significant domestic commitments on climate change. In September 2009, in the run-up to Copenhagen, China pledged to increase the share of non-fossil energy – hydropower, nuclear power, and renewables including wind and solar – to around 15 percent of its energy mix by 2020. That November, the State Council announced that carbon intensity (CO_2 emissions per unit of GDP) would be reduced by 40–45 percent below 2005 levels by 2020. The fact that China made these high-profile voluntary commitments, however, did not mean that it was prepared to accept a legally binding climate treaty. On the contrary, these domestic commitments bolstered the country's argument that it was already doing its part and therefore need not be subject to international obligations.

At the December 2009 Copenhagen summit, China refused to accept any binding international limits on its greenhouse gas emissions.[20] It even blocked a pledge by developed countries to cut their emissions by 80 percent by 2050, afraid that such a target might put indirect pressure on China to provide the remaining emission cuts needed to meet the agreement's goal of limiting global temperature rise to 2 degrees Celsius or less.[21] Tensions flared, especially between the United States and China on the issue of international monitoring, reporting, and verification of CO_2 emissions.

China's position angered many Western governments and observers, who blamed China for the global community's failure in Copenhagen to reach a legally binding climate agreement. But the Chinese government was reportedly satisfied that the Copenhagen Accord preserved the principle of "common but differentiated responsibilities" between developed and developing countries.[22]

The Paris Agreement turnaround

Following the Copenhagen summit, it seemed that there was no way to reconcile the fundamental political differences that were so vividly on display there, especially between the United States and China. A global climate agreement seemed out of reach. Yet only a few years later, in November

2014, during President Obama's visit to Beijing, Presidents Xi and Obama issued an historic Joint Announcement on Climate Change, emphasizing their shared commitment to reaching an ambitious climate agreement in Paris, unveiling their countries' respective climate commitments under the Paris Agreement (including the US commitment to reduce its GHG emissions by 26–28 percent by 2025, compared to 2005 levels, and China's commitment to peak its carbon emissions by around 2030), and expanding US–China cooperation on climate and clean energy. In September 2015, during President Xi's visit to Washington, DC, and just before the Paris climate negotiations, the two presidents issued a follow-up statement that reflected a breakthrough on several key points in the climate negotiations, and highlighted the domestic actions each country was taking to reduce its emissions, as well as continued bilateral climate cooperation efforts.

In contrast to the Copenhagen meeting in 2009, China was widely credited with playing a constructive role in reaching the Paris Agreement in December 2015. As part of its Nationally Determined Contribution (NDC), the post-2020 climate actions that each party to the Agreement intends to achieve, China for the first time pledged to peak its carbon emissions by around 2030 and make best efforts to peak them earlier, a commitment previously unimaginable. And it committed to increase the share of non-fossil energy in its energy mix to 20 percent by 2030. Meeting this pledge will require building an additional 800–1000 gigawatts (GW) of non-fossil energy, roughly equivalent to *the entire US electricity system*. China further pledged to reduce its carbon intensity by 60–65 percent below 2005 levels by 2030 and expand forested land. It also agreed to the establishment of a common system of transparency for countries to report emissions and track progress in meeting their climate commitments, with flexibility to be provided to developing countries, that need it in light of their capacities.

In a third joint statement in March 2016, China and the United States announced their intention to join the Paris Agreement as soon as possible, officially acknowledging their decision in a formal ceremony that September in Hangzhou, China, ahead of the G20 Summit. This show of leadership by the world's two largest emitters paved the way for the rapid entry into force of the Paris Agreement in November 2016.

China's Climate Diplomacy

What changed between Copenhagen and Paris?

China's underlying negotiation principles – protecting its national interest, safeguarding national sovereignty, and enhancing its international image – have remained constant through decades of climate negotiations. What changed between Copenhagen and Paris was how China applied those principles.

Protecting China's national interest

First, and most important, a monumental shift in China's economic development model, triggered by environmental concerns, led the country's leaders to realize that combating climate change is very much in the country's own economic and national interest. For decades, since the start of the program of reforms and opening up of the country to foreign investment in 1978, China's leaders placed economic growth at the top of the national agenda. Provincial governors and city mayors, who relied on Beijing for career advancement and bonuses, were rated primarily on how much they increased local investment and GDP. The national economy boomed as more than 800 million people were lifted out of poverty and a large and growing middle class developed.

But the way in which China achieved this economic miracle – a development model based on export manufacturing and highly polluting heavy industry powered by cheap and abundant coal – was unsustainable, and left a trail of environmental devastation in its wake. A single-minded focus on GDP growth was no longer enough to ensure a better way of life for Chinese citizens. Beginning in the mid-2000s under President Hu Jintao, China's government began to strengthen environmental laws and policies, setting specific targets for air and water pollution reduction and energy efficiency improvements, requiring polluters to disclose air and water pollution data, and enacting a law to support the development of renewable energy in 2005.

Even so, China's environmental situation continued to worsen, as highlighted by severe air pollution outbreaks during the winters of 2011–12 and 2012–13. When President Xi became Communist Party Secretary in November 2012, he stressed that the country's future prosperity depended on a more balanced, equitable, and inclusive development model that protected the environment and people's health – a vision known as "ecological civilization." The party constitution and development plan were amended to note that "the development of ecological civilisation should be integrated into all aspects and the whole process of economic development, political development, cultural development and social development."[23]

This emphasis on ecological civilization coincided with a period of slower economic growth that China's leaders dubbed "the new normal"; rather than emphasizing double-digit growth, the government began to focus on slower, but higher-quality and more balanced, economic growth. Under President Xi, China began to accelerate its efforts to transform its economic structure from one reliant on fossil fuel-driven heavy industry and manufacturing to one based on services, innovation, clean energy, and environmental sustainability.

In December 2013, the central government announced that GDP growth would no longer be the most important factor when evaluating an official's performance. The evaluation criteria would also focus on the quality and sustainability of economic development, including progress in reducing emissions. Hainan province took this a step farther, announcing that an official's environmental record would be the *primary* criterion for promotion decisions. Going even further, in January 2015, Shanghai became the first major region in China to drop its GDP growth targets altogether.

China's Climate Diplomacy

The airpocalypse

A tectonic shift occurred in January 2013, when a weeks-long bout of severe air pollution across northern China demonstrated unmistakably that the country was choking on its own high-speed and unbalanced development. As toxic smog enveloped Beijing and more than 30 other cities, the air quality was at times worse than that in a US airport smoking lounge. In Beijing, air quality monitors recorded concentrations of PM 2.5, the smallest and deadliest air pollutant, of up to 993 micrograms per cubic meter, nearly 40 times the World Health Organization's 24-hour guideline of up to 25 micrograms per cubic meter.[24] People wore face masks to go outside. Hospital admissions soared. Studies showed that air pollution was killing an average of 4,000 people a day – as if "every man, woman and child in China smoked 1.5 cigarettes every hour."[25] China's air pollution crisis attracted global media attention and triggered public outrage throughout the country.

In a break from previous practice, when air pollution was rarely acknowledged, China's domestic media began to cover the "airpocalypse" story. The government had begun releasing hourly air pollution data for more than 70 Chinese cities at the beginning of 2013, and the data showed that almost 92 percent of cities failed to meet the national annual PM 2.5 pollution standard of 35 micrograms per cubic meter.[26] The Ministry of Environmental Protection (now the Ministry of Ecology and Environment) later extended this real-time air quality monitoring program to 338 of China's largest cities. Public concern about air pollution soared. By the end of September, the government had pledged 1.7 trillion renminbi (RMB) to clean the air, and enacted a comprehensive Air Pollution Prevention and Control Action Plan.

Why was the 2013 air pollution crisis a turning point for the Chinese government? Air pollution had been climbing for years, along with the country's coal consumption and vehicle use. What changed, however, was that, for the first time, policymakers and the public could see air pollution data in real time and therefore understand the devastating impact smog was having on public health. The resulting public outcry led the government to make cleaning up deadly pollution a top priority, as well as an integral goal of its new economic development model.

Mounting concerns about climate risks
China's concerns about its own vulnerability to climate change were also growing stronger. In December 2015, during the Paris summit, China

released a 900-page Third National Climate Change Assessment report.[27] Authored by more than 550 scientists and experts, the report painted a dire picture of more frequent and treacherous flooding, droughts, and heat waves. It described how climate change was threatening China's economic centers, as well as major infrastructure projects like the Three Gorges Dam and the Tibetan railroad. It also explained how water shortages caused by melting glaciers in western China could trigger international conflicts over water resources and increase transnational migration.

Recognizing the country's increasing vulnerability to climate change, China also published, in November 2013, a National Strategy for Climate Change Adaptation.[28] This report laid out a comprehensive set of guidelines, targets, and measures to protect water and soil resources and reduce climate impacts on agriculture. It also called for strengthening China's ability to prevent and monitor climate disasters through the establishment of early-warning monitoring and information-sharing systems. The coastal cities with the largest at-risk populations globally from rising sea levels caused by climate change are located in China, including Shanghai, Guangzhou, and Shenzhen.[29] Recognizing this, Shanghai is working to improve its climate resilience and reduce flooding risks by constructing a system of levees, seawalls, and upgraded drainage pipes, and developing an advanced flood information control system.[30]

Public concern about climate change is also mounting. A 2012 survey of public attitudes toward climate change revealed that the majority of Chinese citizens understand that climate change is happening, that it is mainly caused by human activity, and that it is harming China, especially rural residents.[31] They strongly support Chinese government policies addressing climate change.

Public awareness and concern about climate change, as well as support for China's efforts to control GHG emissions, were even stronger when the survey was repeated in 2017.[32] Nearly 80 percent of respondents say they are "very" or "somewhat" worried about climate change. Over 75 percent have already personally experienced the impacts of climate change. Although most people still believe that the government should take the lead in responding to climate change, they are increasingly willing to take action on their own. Nearly three-quarters would be willing to pay more for climate-friendly products, and one-quarter would be willing to pay 200 RMB (about $30) per year to offset their personal emissions. The sharing economy offers more opportunities for the public to participate in climate change action. Over 90 percent of respondents, for example, support using shared bicycles, a model that Chinese companies such as Mobike and Ofo have innovated and pioneered, as a means of travel.

Even though air pollution is still a greater concern to the public, nearly three-quarters of the survey respondents believe that climate change and air pollution are interrelated. So does the Chinese government. As explained by Minister Xie Zhenhua, China's special representative for climate change affairs: "The cause of air pollution and climate change is the same – the burning of fossil fuel. Many of the policies and measures to solve the two issues are also the same, such as reducing coal consumption."[33]

By the time of the Paris climate negotiations in December 2015, China recognized that measures to address climate change and air pollution were not only aligned with the country's economic restructuring goals, but were also valuable tools for helping to reach those goals. China's leaders also understood that clean technology offers the largest market opportunity of the twenty-first century. As Gao Feng, former special representative for climate change negotiations in the Ministry of Foreign Affairs, explained: "We need a new industry that is powerful enough to drive the economy, on a more sustainable and cleaner basis . . . We are fairly confident that climate change and environmental protection will become a powerful new driver of the economy."[34]

This statement provides a clear illustration of how China's climate diplomacy has evolved since the days of the Beijing Declaration. The country's climate negotiators are still working to protect China's foreign policy and economic interests. The difference now is that they recognize that combating climate change is very much in China's own national interest.

Safeguarding national sovereignty

Another major reason for the change in China's climate diplomacy was the hybrid architecture of the Paris Agreement itself. Even though the Agreement is legally binding, many of its provisions are not, including individual country commitments and NDCs. Rather than the top-down approach that countries tried and failed to negotiate at Copenhagen, the Paris Agreement uses a "pledge and review" system, in which countries make climate commitments based on their own political and economic circumstances and national interests. The Paris Agreement rules requiring each country to regularly report on its climate actions and greenhouse gas emissions provide a "peer-pressure" mechanism for motivating each country to implement its own commitments.

This is in many ways the type of system that China has been championing for decades, although including the NDCs in the framework of the legally binding Agreement confers many more political and social obligations on countries to meet their pledges than if they were purely domestic commitments. The major downside of this approach, of course, is that the total of all the country pledges made to date is nowhere near what is needed to meet the Agreement's goals, requiring countries to regularly strengthen their commitments over time.

Enhancing China's international image

Although Donald Trump has abdicated America's climate leadership, Xi Jinping has taken the opposite approach, making international cooperation on climate change an important element of his foreign policy. He has promised to provide financial and technical support to other developing countries in reducing their emissions and adapting to climate change, including establishing a 20 billion RMB ($3.1 billion) South-South Climate Cooperation Fund. He has also pledged to get "actively involved in global environmental governance."[35] These actions have helped to burnish

China's international image as a proponent of strong international climate action.

But for China, the world's largest GHG emitter, to truly become a "torchbearer" in global climate change efforts, it first needs to meet and exceed its own Paris pledges, and then strengthen its commitments over time. How fast can the country push its own carbon emissions to peak, and at what level? The answer comes down to coal.

2

Dethroning Old King Coal

When my family and I lived in Beijing in the early 1990s, winter meant coal. Each year on November 15, regardless of the weather, the government switched on the coal-fired central heating system in the nation's capital and in other cities throughout northern China. The skies would darken and our clothes and faces would become covered with soot. Mountains of coal were stockpiled on the street. Looking out our grimy apartment window, I would see people pedaling three-wheeled bicycles laden with chunks of coal to their homes in Beijing's ancient *hutongs* for use in heating and cooking. In the distance loomed the belching smokestacks of four coal-fired power plants and Beijing's Capital Steel Factory (also referred to as the Shougang Group), then the largest steel mill in the country.

Beijing has come a long way since then. Beginning with its efforts to host a "Green Olympics" in 2008 and accelerating after the 2013 air pollution crisis, the city has invested billions of RMB to kick its addiction to coal. It has converted all its heating and power facilities from coal to natural gas, closed nearly 2,000 factories, and moved the Capital Steel Factory behemoth to nearby Hebei province. The capital closed its last coal plant in March 2017.

Yet despite recent improvements, the air in Beijing remains heavily polluted, in part because it is surrounded by the country's coal and heavy industry heartland. As Greenpeace put it, "more coal [was] consumed [in 2011] within 600 kilometers of China's capital than in the entire United States."[1] Much of this coal was burned in Hebei province, the world's largest steel manufacturer, which produced more steel in 2014 than any country other than China itself. Hebei also produces half of the world's glass panels, 60 percent of the world's cement, and two-thirds of the world's aluminum.

For decades, China relied on cheap and abundant coal to power its economic miracle. During its 2000–13 economic boom, coal consumption tripled from 1.4 billion tons to 4.24 billion tons a year, to the point where it was burning as much coal as the rest of the world combined.[2] From 2000 to

2015, about 724 GW of coal-fired power generation capacity was built, the largest such expansion in human history.[3]

China's addiction to coal has come at an enormous cost. What Donald Trump calls "beautiful, clean coal" is in fact the world's dirtiest and most carbon-intensive fossil fuel, producing the least energy and the most pollution per kilogram of any fuel.[4] Coal is the single largest source of air pollution in China, contributing 93 percent of its sulfur dioxide (SO_2) emissions, over 70 percent of its nitrogen oxides (NOx) emissions, and more than 60 percent of its fine particulate matter emissions, known as PM 2.5, the most dangerous form of air pollution.[5] Experts have estimated that coal was responsible for 708,000 premature deaths in China in 2012 due to cardiopulmonary disease. Another study calculated that the average life expectancy for people in northern China, who burn coal for heat during the winter and who therefore experience high levels of air pollution, was 5.5 years shorter than for those in southern China.[6]

Coal is not just the largest source of air pollution in China. It also produces 80 percent of the country's energy sector CO_2 emissions. This means that China's coal consumption is the largest single source of CO_2 emissions in the world, responsible on its own for about 7.2 billion tons per year, more than the total emissions from any other country. Reining in coal is therefore the most crucial step China can take to protect the health of its people, preserve its precious natural resources, and save the country and the planet from the devastating impacts of climate change.

China's war on coal

The urgent need to tackle air pollution and reduce CO_2 emissions, along with the plunging cost of renewables, is pushing China to rebalance its economy and shift away from coal-fired heavy industry. The major tool in the war on coal is strong, top-down policymaking.

China's 2013 "airpocalypse" triggered the first wave of government measures aimed squarely at reducing coal consumption in the most polluted regions. In September 2013, China's State Council unveiled a four-year Air Pollution Prevention and Control Action Plan. The goal of the plan was to significantly improve the air quality of the entire country by the end of 2017, with stricter air pollution and coal consumption reduction targets in three key industrial regions surrounding Beijing,

Shanghai, and Guangzhou. These three regions – Beijing/Tianjin/Hebei (BTH), the Yangtze River Delta (YRD), and the Pearl River Delta (PRD) – together account for more than 60 percent of China's GDP and over half of its coal consumption.

In addition to requiring nationwide and regional reductions in major air pollutants, the Action Plan prohibited the approval of new coal-fired power plants in the three key regions, except for combined heat and power plants. It also required the three regions to replace coal with electricity generated from natural gas and non-fossil energy. By 2015, 20 provinces and more than 30 cities had made additional commitments to reduce their coal consumption. These included pledges by the cities of Beijing and Tianjin and the provinces of Hebei and Shandong to cut their coal use in 2017 by a total of 83 million tons, equal to the entire 2012 coal consumption of Canada.

Coal consumption caps

The Action Plan was a welcome and major step forward in tackling China's air pollution crisis. By focusing on cutting regional and local air pollution, however, it carried the risk of pollution and carbon "leakage," providing an incentive for coal companies to move operations to less polluted and less regulated parts of the country. To address this issue and to help develop cleaner energy sources, improve air quality, and tackle climate change, NRDC in 2013 launched the China Coal Consumption Cap Plan and Policy Research Project. One of the project's first efforts was in developing and recommending to the central government a comprehensive roadmap and policy package for establishing and implementing a binding nationwide coal consumption cap.

The project brought together leading experts from more than 20 Chinese government think-tanks, research institutes, industry associations, and NGOs. The project team demonstrated, through rigorous research, that accelerating the replacement of coal with cleaner energy sources and implementing energy efficient technologies and practices will fundamentally help China achieve its long-term economic, technological, and environmental goals.

A breakthrough came in January 2017, when China's 13th Five-Year Plan for Energy Development established the nation's first mandatory cap on national coal consumption. The plan requires China to reduce the percentage of coal in the country's total energy mix to no more than 58 percent by 2020, a substantial reduction from coal's 64 percent share in 2015 and levels as high as 70 percent during China's 2000–10 economic boom years. Setting a mandatory coal consumption target is essential: it means that policymakers must strengthen policies and measures to reduce coal consumption and replace it with cleaner alternatives. China is now implementing the coal cap targets in industries, provinces, and cities.

Shutting down excess industrial capacity

China is also reducing coal consumption by eliminating excess capacity in the smokestack industries, a key goal of the country's economic restructuring efforts. Under the 13th Five-Year Plan, a total of 150 GW of new coal power capacity will be canceled or postponed until at least 2020, although these plants may be restarted after 2020. The plan also requires closure of 20 GW of outdated coal plant capacity, 1.0 billion tons of excess coalmining capacity (with no new coalmine approvals), 100–150 million tons of iron and steel capacity, and 300 million tons of cement capacity. Some Chinese experts believe that with systematic planning and aggressive measures, more could be achieved, retiring a cumulative 50 GW of coal power capacity by 2020 and 200 GW by 2030, thereby avoiding the risk of unneeded coal plants becoming "stranded assets."

Industrial energy efficiency

China has also relied heavily on improving energy efficiency as the most cost-effective means of reducing coal consumption and controlling air pollution from its smokestack industries. Mandatory energy efficiency programs in China's largest and most energy-intensive industries, which have been in place since 2006, have been one of the most effective steps taken by any country to reduce GHG emissions.

Between 2006 and 2014, $370 billion was invested in energy efficiency, mostly in industry, generating energy savings that were as large as China's entire renewable energy supply at that time. According to the International Energy Agency (IEA), such energy efficiency gains in the power sector alone reduced China's CO_2 emissions in 2014 by 1.2 billion tons, equivalent to the total CO_2 emissions of Japan. They also avoided the need for over $230 billion of investments in new (mostly coal-fired) power plants. The 13th Five-Year Plan sets strong energy intensity targets that will drive an expected $270 billion in additional energy efficiency investments by 2020.[7]

Power plant standards

Coal-fired power plants are responsible for about half of China's coal use. Tough efficiency standards now require every existing coal plant to install advanced technology in order to reduce the amount of coal consumed per unit of power produced to 310 grams of coal equivalent per kilowatt hour (kWh) by 2020.[8] The 13th Five-Year Work Plan for Controlling GHG Emissions also requires every large power generation company to ensure that their coal-fired power plants, on average across all their plants, limit CO_2 emissions to no more than 550 grams of CO per kWh by 2020. And in 2014 China established ultra-low emissions standards for coal power plants, requiring them to be as low-polluting as natural gas power plants.

These standards are designed to increase coal plant operating expenses to more fully reflect their environmental costs, putting pressure on companies to phase out their most polluting plants, to upgrade others, and to accelerate the drive toward clean energy. Coal-fired power plants that cannot meet the new efficiency and emissions standards are to be shut down and disconnected from the grid.[9] Plants that do meet the emission standards will receive discounts on their tariff rates.

Carbon trading

In addition to the command-and-control measures described above, China is seeking to expand the role of market forces in driving the transition from coal to clean energy. In December 2017, China made good on its promise to put a price on carbon by launching a national carbon trading program. This move sends a signal that the carbon impact of burning fossil fuels and other industrial activity should be accounted for in business planning and investment decisions. The goal is to push companies to make even greater investments in clean energy in China, which already has the world's largest renewable energy and electric vehicles market.

The national program will build upon and integrate the experiences from China's seven pilot carbon trading programs, which were launched in 2013 in five cities and two provinces. By the end of September 2017, these pilots covered almost 3,000 entities from more than 20 industry sectors. Trading volumes reached 200 million tons of CO_2 equivalent, and trading value was over 45 billion RMB.

The national program will initially cover only the power sector, China's largest source of CO_2 emissions. This sector alone is responsible for one-third of the country's total carbon emissions – about 3.3 billion tons each year – which will make the national program the largest emission trading program in the world. The first two years will be a trial period during which emission allowances will be allocated to individual companies and simulated trading will be conducted. The full program is scheduled to begin in 2020, though many details are not yet available. Over time, however, China will likely expand trading to include eight sectors that are together responsible for half of all the country's emissions.

A successful carbon market requires several key building blocks: an effective management mechanism, robust supporting legislation, a reliable trading system, accurate emission data, and strong capacity at all levels. Based upon the experience of China's pilot programs and other carbon markets, data quality is vital to ensure the integrity of the emission trading system. Most of the 1,700 companies that will be targeted initially in the national program are large state-owned enterprises, which generally have better monitoring capacity than smaller private companies. We expect that China will invest significant resources in obtaining and verifying good emissions data to ensure that companies are reporting their emissions accurately and participating fairly in the program.

The experience of the European Union and several US states in developing carbon trading markets has been instructive. It demonstrates that the process of setting up a robust carbon cap and trading program, and reaching a high enough price on carbon to have a significant impact on business and investment decisions, can take many years. The process will be even more challenging for China, since many sectors of the economy – including the power sector – are still not market-based. China is now undertaking broad power market reforms that will be critical to the effectiveness of the carbon trading market. If they are successful, combining the national coal cap target with a national carbon trading program should accelerate the pace of China's energy transition and clean technology scale-up, and will be important for shifting the economy to a more balanced development.

Government reorganization

In March 2018, China announced a major government reorganization plan that, among other things, expands the responsibilities of the environment ministry, creating a new Ministry of Ecology and Environment. As part of this reorganization, the new ministry will take on the job of managing climate change and GHG emission reduction efforts, which were previously under the jurisdiction of the National Development and Reform Commission.

This move is designed to centralize environmental regulatory policy and enable the MEE to tackle air pollution and GHG emissions in a coordinated manner, using its significant enforcement powers. Some observers question whether the MEE will be powerful enough to carry out its mission. It is clear, however, that China's top leaders intend this move to strengthen the country's environmental protection efforts. In his opening speech to the National People's Congress in March 2018, President Xi pledged that China will "devote more energy and take more concrete measures to advance the building of an ecological civilization, accelerate efforts to develop green production and ways of life, and work harder to tackle prominent environmental problems."

Challenges

But dethroning Old King Coal, as President Xi put it, is "no walk in the park." China faces unprecedented challenges in shifting the world's second largest economy away from heavy industry, cutting air pollution, and reducing carbon emissions while ensuring sustained economic growth. It must also deal with pushback from those who benefit from smokestack industries or stand to lose under the "new normal": displaced workers, local governments, and the coal industry itself.

Displaced workers

Millions of workers are losing jobs in smokestack industries during China's economic transition. The Minister of Human Resources said in 2016 that the reductions in excess industrial production capacity through 2020 would eliminate 1.3 million jobs in the coal sector and another 500,000 in the steel industry. Some experts forecast that 5–6 million workers could eventually be laid off.[10] The government has set aside a $15 billion fund to relocate and retrain laid-off workers, and has encouraged firms and local governments to help find new jobs for them, including in the services sector, which is growing rapidly.

Making this transition, however, is easier said than done. Many coal and steel workers are reluctant to switch to lower-paying service jobs, to adjust to a new way of life, or to move from communities where few other jobs are currently available. They must compete with 15 million young people entering the workforce each year. Much of the retraining and resettlement fund to date has been used to cover back pay for workers in debt-ridden state-owned enterprises.[11]

The good news is that China's transition to a cleaner, low-carbon economy offers major new employment opportunities in renewable energy and energy efficiency. China already leads the world in clean energy jobs, with 3.64 million jobs in 2016 in solar, wind, and other clean energy sectors.[12] It expects to generate another *13 million* new clean energy jobs by 2020.[13] Fully implementing the national cap on coal consumption would accelerate this process after 2020, creating more jobs than those lost in the coal industry.[14]

Green buildings, for example, offer major new employment opportunities. When I launched NRDC's clean energy program in China in the mid-1990s, there were no green buildings anywhere in the country. In 1999, however, my colleague Rob Watson and I were asked to coordinate China's first green building demonstration project, which was jointly sponsored by the US Department of Energy and China's Ministry of Science and Technology. The project, the Agenda 21 building in Beijing, broke ground in 2002, and the building's official opening ceremony took place in February 2004.

The building earned the Leadership in Energy and Environmental Design (LEED) Gold Certificate, becoming the first internationally certified green building in China. The building employs high-efficiency heating, cooling, and lighting technologies to use 72 percent less energy and 40 percent less water than typical new office buildings in Beijing, expending 1,900 fewer tons of carbon pollution per year. Convinced that something was amiss, the local government installed cages around the building's meters to prevent tampering, but the dramatic results continued. In recognition of the project's success in demonstrating the feasibility of green buildings in China, the Ministry of Construction (now the Ministry of Housing and Urban-Rural Development) awarded NRDC its first international Green Building Innovation Award.

Since the construction of the Agenda 21 building, China has become the largest building construction market in the world, accounting for half of all new build globally. The government has mandated that much of this construction must be green, so that buildings reduce their energy and water footprint. The 13th Five-Year Plan for Building Energy Efficiency and Green Building Development includes a requirement that 50 percent of all new urban buildings in the country must be certified green. The plan also calls for pilot programs to renovate primary and secondary schools, community hospitals, and public buildings so they become more energy efficient. Nearly 20 cities have set even more ambitious building efficiency targets.[15]

Retraining technically skilled workers to take advantage of these new opportunities could be a win-win-win situation for the workers, their communities, and the environment. It could also play a key role in China's low-carbon drive. Buildings are the fastest-growing source of energy consumption and CO_2 emissions in China and could account for as much as 40 percent of total energy consumption in the next 15 years as the country continues to urbanize.

Local governments

Another major obstacle to China's war on coal is the resistance of local government officials. Coal has been the backbone of the country's economy for decades, and some regions have been completely dependent on the coal economy. Mammoth iron and steel factories and coal-fired power plants have long provided secure jobs and filled local government coffers with tax revenues. In the days when China had a completely planned economy, these state-owned enterprises often also provided their workers with free housing, free transportation, and even free medical treatment. Provincial governors and city mayors, who report to the central government, were rated for decades solely on how well they grew their GDP. Many local officials were therefore able to succeed and prosper in the smokestack economy, even as factories poisoned the air and water with toxic chemicals, destroyed farm-land, and decimated natural resources.

As a result, even as China's top leaders work to curb the country's reliance on coal, many local government officials have pushed back. Anxious to expand their tax base and attract new jobs, and knowing that a clampdown on coal-fired power was coming, local officials have rushed to approve new coal-fired power plants in the last few years, even though few if any of them are needed.

This flood of new coal plants does not necessarily translate into an increase in CO_2 emissions. Instead, as power demand growth slows under the "new normal" economy, and the share of renewable energy and low-carbon generation continues to grow, coal-fired power plants are running for fewer and fewer hours. In 2016, the average utilization rate for the nation's coal plants was under 50 percent, meaning that China's coal plants stood idle for half the time.

Yet these new plants still represent a threat to China's low-carbon transition. If investment in coal is not restrained, by 2030 these plants could represent $90.4 billion worth of "stranded coal assets" – plants that will never make a return on investment.[16] This would place heavy pressure on the government to find ways to keep these plants in operation during their 40–50-year lifetime.

In 2017, recognizing these risks, Beijing placed 24 of its 31 provinces on "red alert," ordering them to stop approving new coal-fired power plants because of severe overcapacity or environmental risks.[17] It put another four provinces on "orange alert." Only two provinces – Hunan and Hainan – received a green light for new coal investments. Local governments, which have been known to reopen plants secretly even after they have been ordered to close them by the central government, may still find a way around these "red traffic light" prohibitions. And red alerts for some provinces were lifted in 2018. But this program is a welcome sign that Beijing is working to stem the tide of unneeded coal plants.

The coal industry

Many of China's coal provinces and coal enterprises are seeking ways to diversify as the country transitions from coal to clean energy. Shanxi province, the coalmining heartland of China, is promoting the development of tourism, solar power plants, and cellphone manufacturing as alternative industries. In June 2017, Anhui province turned on the world's largest floating solar power plant, which sits on a lake over a collapsed coalmine. The solar plant will produce enough electricity to power 15,000 homes.[18]

Some coal companies are also expanding into the booming wind and solar industries. Others, however, are seeking to develop dangerous new coal-to-chemical or coal gasification industries, which could threaten precious water resources and cause CO_2 emissions to skyrocket. Converting coal to oil or gas requires large amounts of coal, emitting more than three times as much CO_2 as mining and using conventional oil and gas. The coal-to-gas process also requires far more water than traditional coalmining, posing a significant risk, since many of these plants are being planned in northwestern China, the country's most water-stressed region.

Though the current "modern" coal chemicals industry is small, it could grow dramatically if unchecked. If current plants are approved, coal consumption from this industry could skyrocket from 90 million tons in 2015 to more than 400 million tons by 2020.[19] The government has banned the construction of any coal-to-gas plants that would produce fewer than 2 billion cubic meters of gas per year. But it has not yet issued any definitive guidance on whether and how it would allow this industry to grow, posing a significant risk to China's decarbonization drive.

Enforcement

Enforcement of environmental regulations has long been a challenge in China. Yet in recent years powerful new enforcement tools that are starting to make a difference have been put in the hands of environmental officials and the public.

In 2015, China amended its bedrock Environmental Protection Law (EPL) to, among other things, establish a game-changing new environmental penalty system. The previous system imposed one-off fines that amounted to little more than a slap on the wrist of environmental polluters. Under the new penalty system, modeled after that of the United States, fines continue to accumulate for each day the pollution violations continue. This system has greatly increased the cost of pollution and improved compliance.

From January to December 2015, the first year the new system was in effect, local environmental protection bureaus brought 715 environmental penalty cases nationwide, resulting in total fines of approximately $95 million. In January 2018, the government successfully fined two Chinese truckmakers a total of at least $5.8 million for manufacturing vehicles that did not meet emission standards and for engaging in emissions fraud.[20] This was the largest fine against vehicle manufacturers as a result of violations of China's amended Air Pollution Prevention and Control Law.

China also increasingly recognizes that public participation and open information are essential features of any successful environmental enforcement system. The 13th Five-Year Plan requires polluting enterprises to comprehensively disclose all emissions data online to enable effective monitoring. All of China's provincial-level environmental agencies have developed online disclosure platforms for key polluters. The MEE now periodically discloses a list of enterprises with serious violations of emission requirements based on this online monitoring data.

The Institute of Public & Environmental Affairs (IPE), a Chinese NGO, has launched a "Blue Map" online app that provides the public with access to real-time environmental information and emissions data from 9,000 polluting enterprises.[21] The IPE's database, which collects disclosed enforcement information and emission data, is linked to China's Green Finance Committee and the China Finance Information Website, so that banks and other financial institutions can evaluate a company's environmental compliance record for purposes of risk evaluation.

My organization, NRDC, has worked with judges, lawyers, government officials, and other environmental groups for nearly two decades to strengthen China's environmental laws and their enforcement, and to encourage public environmental awareness and stewardship. We have also worked with the All-China Lawyers Association and the Harvard Law School Negotiation and Mediation Clinic to train lawyers to resolve environmental disputes through negotiation, and shared the US experience with public interest environmental lawsuits to help enforce pollution standards against polluters.

The 2015 EPL amendments allow NGOs to take legal action against polluters on behalf of the public interest. In 2015, the first year these amendments were in effect, 36 civil environmental public interest litigation cases and 6 administrative environmental public interest litigation cases were filed. By November 2015, 24 provinces had established 456 environmental and/or natural resources tribunals, collegial panels, and circuit courts. All levels of the People's Court have actively accepted and tried these environmental public interest cases.

In July 2016, the All-China Environment Federation (ACEF), a Chinese environmental NGO, won the country's first public interest lawsuit aimed at air pollution. The defendant, a glass-making factory in Shandong province, had to pay $2.9 million in compensation and issue a public apology for damaging the health of local residents with its toxic air emissions. The court accepted ACEF's assessment of the environmental damages caused by these emissions, which will make it easier to bring air pollution cases in the future.

Results

China's war on coal has already begun to demonstrate impressive results, raising hopes that carbon emissions may peak years before the 2030 pledge. After growing by an average of 10 percent annually from 2002 to 2012, China's coal consumption leveled off in 2013 and decreased in each of the following three years. Because China is responsible for nearly half of the world's coal consumption, the impact was significant. The IEA said that global coal demand decreased in 2015 for the first time in this century.[22] In addition, largely because of the dip in China's coal consumption, global CO_2 emissions growth was basically flat between 2014 and 2016, even as the economy continued to grow.

But China's low-carbon transition still faces a bumpy road, at least in the near term. After three years of decline, coal consumption jumped by 3 percent through the first three-quarters of 2017, alarming experts and policymakers. The major reason was a government stimulus package that boosted investment in infrastructure. But by focusing the stimulus on infrastructure, rather than on social expenditures and transfers (as recommended by the International Monetary Fund), the stimulus spurred production in coal-intensive industries such as iron and steel and coal power, the very sectors of the economy that China is trying to scale down. It stalled the country's transition to a "new normal" of lower but higher-quality growth, and exacerbated the structural problems facing China's industrial economy, including severe overcapacity and rising debt.

The stimulus also sent coal consumption and air pollution soaring once more. Levels of hazardous PM 2.5 pollution were again off the charts. Visibility was down to 50 meters in some parts of northern China. This was especially problematic because all the targets in the national Air Pollution Action Plan were due to be met by the end of 2017. The 19th Communist Party Congress, an event held only once every five years to select the party's top leadership, was also scheduled for October 2017 in Beijing. Meeting the air pollution targets therefore carried additional political significance.

The central government swung into action, launching an end-of-year "battle plan" that brought coal consumption to a screeching halt in northern China, the country's coal heartland. The government suspended major construction projects and shut down dozens of steel mills and cement plants. This was the largest shutdown in history, affecting one-quarter of China's total steel-making capacity and about 10 percent of its cement production.[23]

For the first time, China also tackled coal use in rural homes and small industrial boilers. Replacing these small-scale coal uses with natural gas and electric heating is a costly, time-consuming process. But the government wanted immediate results, so it required the 28 cities in and around the BTH region to replace coal heating systems by the end of October.

The results illustrate both the decisiveness and the limits of China's command-and-control system, especially when carried out without adequate planning or sufficient input from residents and other stakeholders. Some local government officials followed orders to remove coal stoves and boilers, but were slow to install natural gas pipelines and heaters. Demand for natural gas soared, leading to shortages, price spikes, and supply interruptions. Thousands of households, even whole villages, were left without heat amid freezing winter temperatures. The government ultimately lifted the coal ban in areas where stable and affordable natural gas supplies were not yet available.

In the long run, efforts to address this "dispersed coal" use, if carried out correctly, can provide major benefits in terms of improved air quality and public health. The BTH region ultimately replaced coal heating with gas or electric heating in about 3.24 million households in 2017, reducing coal use by 8 million tons.[24] When combined with China's other air pollution control efforts, the results were dramatic. By the end of the year, Beijing experienced its biggest improvement in air quality in at least nine years. Average levels of pollutants fell about 35 percent from 2012 numbers, with nearly half the improvement taking place in 2017.[25]

Because of the all-out efforts to reduce and replace coal with gas and electric heating in the last quarter of 2017, China's annual coal consumption ultimately increased by only 0.4 percent for the whole of that year, with CO_2 emissions rising by 1.4 percent, according to official data. This is a lot less than what many predicted based on the first three-quarters of rapid growth, and still below coal's 2013 peak. Many experts believe the recent increase in coal consumption is a temporary one. But the dramatic shifts in coal use in 2017 illustrate some of the formidable challenges facing China's leaders in their quest to restructure and decarbonize the economy. And coal consumption began to rise again in 2018 as the infrastructure-based economic stimulus continued.

Despite these challenges, it seems clear that Old King Coal is on its way out in China, despite short-term fluctuations. Coal's share in China's power generation dropped from 80 percent in 2010 to 60 percent in 2017. Between 2013 and 2017, coal consumption was reduced by 380 million tons. By the end of 2017, carbon intensity had fallen by 47 percent below 2005 levels, meeting the 2020 Copenhagen carbon intensity reduction target three years ahead of schedule. Some Chinese experts believe that China's carbon emissions are still on track to peak as early as 2020, ten years ahead of its Paris pledge.

The country's structural transformation, its air pollution control imperative, and its commitment to meeting its climate pledges will continue to drive coal's inexorable decline. But there's more to the story than China's war on coal. China's leadership is also driving a clean energy revolution that is hastening coal's demise, not just at home, but throughout the world.

3

Catalyzing the Clean Energy Revolution

In March 2010, I helped organize a trip to China for a group of Stanford University students who were studying China's energy systems. In addition to visiting a 900 MW coal-fired power plant in Shanghai and touring the Three Gorges Dam, the world's largest hydroelectric plant, we went to Dezhou, a city with a population of 5 million located along the main rail route between Beijing and Shanghai. A man there named Huang Ming, owner of one of China's largest solar water heater companies, had begun to build his dream: the largest solar energy production base in the world. He named the $740 million project Solar Valley, after Silicon Valley in California.

We stayed at his centerpiece project, a giant wedge-shaped, multistory hotel covered with solar-thermal hot water heaters and solar photovoltaic

(PV) panels. A demonstration center featured a Rube Goldberg-like assortment of experimental solar technologies. Factories, research labs, and a solar college were under construction. It even boasted a solar museum, which later that year acquired one of the solar hot water panels that then-US President Jimmy Carter had installed on the roof of the White House in 1979 and that Ronald Reagan later removed.[1]

Huang Ming and his company, Himin Solar, did not initially have any real expertise in solar photovoltaic technologies. Solar-thermal water heaters operate on very different physical principles. But, as explained by Stanford lecturer Kevin Hsu, who helped to lead the trip:

> Himin exemplifies Chinese businesses' willingness to dream big – and they are not afraid to let you know about it. Whether they actually achieve these goals or not, they see transformative action as a kind of calling. It's not clear if this is a marketing ploy, an attempt to search for the "next big thing" in their sector, or if they simply have no clear strategy for growth, so they hope to "do it all" to scale up.[2]

By the time of our visit, China, the world's manufacturing base, had already become the leading manufacturer of solar panels, accounting for 50 percent of total global production. But 90 percent of these panels were being exported overseas to countries like Germany that already had well-established solar subsidy programs up and running. In contrast, China's domestic solar power industry was virtually nonexistent. Reporting on Himin's Solar Valley at the time, the *Washington Post* was dubious: "Short of a calamitous economic collapse or a game-changing technological breakthrough, China's chances look slim: Its mostly coal- and oil-fueled economy is growing so fast that its real but relatively modest green gains simply can't keep up." The *Post* quoted a Tsinghua University professor, who said the "manufacturing of solar devices helps local economies but won't break or even dent China's reliance on carbon-rich fossil fuels."[3]

Little did we know how fast that was about to change. In 2007, the country's fledgling solar PV industry had only installed 100 megawatts (MW) of domestic capacity, mostly in rural areas far from the grid. This amount is less than is currently installed in the city of San Antonio, Texas.[4] Then the 2008 global financial crisis hit. International demand for solar panels plummeted as Western countries cut back their solar subsidies, adding to an existing glut in Chinese-manufactured solar panels and wreaking havoc on the industry. The government responded with a raft of measures designed to create a domestic market for its solar cell and panel manufacturers.

Among other moves, China amended its 2005 Renewable Energy Law in 2009 to require grid companies to purchase a fixed share of their power generation from renewable energy sources. This requirement is similar to the Renewable Portfolio Standards (RPS) in effect in many Western countries and 29 of the 50 US states, though enforcement in China has been notably lax. The law requires grid companies to be compensated for the higher cost of purchasing wind and solar power through a renewable energy surcharge on end-use energy consumers.

In the run-up to the 2009 Copenhagen climate summit, China pledged to increase the share of non-fossil fuels to around 15 percent of its energy mix by 2020. To jumpstart these efforts, China launched a solar roofs subsidy program, as well as a $3 billion "Golden Sun" initiative which subsidized 50–70 percent of the investment and grid connection costs of hundreds of solar power installations across the country. By the end of 2010, the first full year of the Golden Sun program, China's total PV installed capacity grew by 166 percent from the year before, to nearly 900 MW, the equivalent of one large coal-fired power plant.[5]

China's domestic wind power industry was already up and running, taking advantage of the country's abundant wind resources, which are similar in scale to those in the United States, though mostly concentrated in northern and western regions far from demand centers. China built its wind industry through a combination of measures, including government financing, demonstration projects, market-based mechanisms such as competitive bidding, government-approved tariffs, and national targets. In 2004, it also imposed a "local content" requirement (abolished in 2010) that wind farms had to buy equipment in which at least 70 percent of the value was domestically manufactured. These measures helped push wind power capacity in China to more than double every year from 2006 to 2009.[6]

In 2009, China established a national feed-in tariff (FIT) for wind and, in 2011, a national FIT for solar PV. FITs are powerful policy tools used in many countries to encourage deployment of renewable energy technologies. A FIT guarantees renewable energy generators a fixed purchase price for each kWh they produce and "feed-into" the grid. In order to compensate wind and solar power generators for the higher costs of zero-carbon renewable technologies until they scale up and reach "grid parity" with coal power, the fixed price is higher than the cost of coal-fired power. To finance the solar and wind FITs and other special renewable energy projects, China created a national Renewable Energy Subsidy Fund, supported by a surcharge on energy consumers and other government funding sources.

To implement the FITs, China's National Energy Administration (NEA) sets annual quotas by province for new solar and wind capacity, along with the FIT rates to be applied that year. The NEA also issues an annual list of specific projects that are eligible to begin receiving the FITs. The NEA has been gradually reducing FIT rates as the cost of new wind and solar projects drops. This, however, has led to a periodic rush of new project applications by developers hoping to qualify for FIT rates before they are reduced, whether or not the new plants are located near energy demand centers or even able to connect to the grid. It has also put pressure on the government to increase power prices in order to cover the estimated $19 billion deficit in the Renewable Energy Subsidy Fund.

The NEA hopes to eventually replace the FIT system with a new Green Electricity Certificate program in which coal-fired power plants must buy "certificates" from renewable energy suppliers. A voluntary pilot project, launched in July 2017, is off to a slow start, but the NEA plans to make it compulsory for new wind and solar plants as soon as possible. The NEA is also developing a renewable energy obligation policy that will require provinces to obtain a certain percentage of their electricity from renewable energy.

The 12th Five-Year Plan (2011–15) designated solar and wind manufacturing as "strategic industries" chosen to drive the country's economic modernization and enhance its global competitiveness. For wind power, which was already booming domestically, the plan called for the development of eight major onshore bases, the construction of small and medium-sized wind farms in regions of the country with better access to the grid, and development of offshore wind projects.

For solar power, a special five-year plan laid out a comprehensive and highly detailed strategy designed to strengthen China's solar PV industry, reduce costs, improve quality, promote technological innovation, increase R&D, and expand China's solar market overseas. Each of these goals was accompanied by specific targets, timetables, and policy measures, and later implemented with government funding and financial incentives.

The results have been nothing short of extraordinary, especially for solar. After revising its 2015 target upward several times – from 5 to 10 to 35 GW – China smashed them all, bringing its total solar PV installed capacity to 43 GW in 2015, and overtaking Germany as the world's leading solar PV country. In 2016, China added an additional world record 34 GW of solar capacity, far outpacing every other country. China's additions in 2016 contributed almost half the growth in global solar PV capacity that year.

Experts predicted that China's solar market would slow in 2017, but the government did not decrease FIT rates as much as predicted. Nor did it move to stop the construction of projects above approved provincial quotas. In addition, as the cost of solar continued to fall, many large energy consumers installed their own solar panels on rooftops and industrial parks. The government encourages these type of projects, known as distributed solar, which are not limited by quotas.

This combination of factors led to an even more astonishing result: nearly 53 GW of additional solar PV capacity was installed in 2017. This means that China installed more solar capacity in one year than the *total, cumulative solar capacity of any other country* as of the end of 2016.[7] In fact, China built more solar power in 2017 than any other energy source, including coal, with solar accounting for half of all new global installed capacity. Every hour, China now erects another wind turbine, and installs enough solar panels to cover a soccer field.[8]

With this unprecedented surge in new solar plants, China brought its total installed capacity to over 130 GW in 2017, surpassing its 2020 solar PV target of 105 GW three years ahead of schedule. The NEA responded by setting new annual targets that together more than double China's previous 2020 target.

The new target, 213 GW, is five times larger than the total solar capacity of the United States in 2017. According to Greenpeace, meeting this target will be comparable to covering an area of land as large as Greater London — 1,500 square kilometers – with solar panels.[9] The IEA estimates that solar PV in China could reach a total of 320 GW by 2022, equivalent to the total electricity capacity of Japan.[10]

Wind power has also continued to take off in China. According to a report by the International Renewable Energy Agency, China installed more wind capacity in the five years from 2007 to 2011 than either the United States or Germany installed in more than 30 years of wind power development.[11] Growth continued at a steady pace of about 30 percent a year from 2010 to 2015. By the end of 2016,

China had installed nearly 105,000 wind turbines, more than one out of every three turbines in the world.[12] Analysts predict that China could triple its 2015 wind energy capacity by 2030, reaching more than 495 GW.[13] By comparison, the global wind capacity in 2016 was around 487 GW.

China's impact on the global clean energy revolution

China recognizes that ramping up clean energy is a crucial strategy for meeting its own climate, environmental, economic restructuring and energy security goals. But there's more to it than that. China also understands that clean energy is the largest new market opportunity of the twenty-first century – and it is determined to lead the way.

China is already the leading manufacturer of renewable energy equipment. Five of the ten largest wind turbine manufacturers and nine of the world's top ten solar panel manufacturers are Chinese owned or operated.[14] In 2017, Chinese solar manufacturers accounted for about 68 percent of global solar cell production and more than 70 percent of the world's production of solar panels, also known as solar modules.

Catalyzing the Clean Energy Revolution

It is very likely that China's lead will continue to expand. In the first half of 2017, the country was responsible for 70 percent of the world's planned solar manufacturing capacity expansions.[15] Chinese firms now have the capacity to manufacture 51 GW of solar PV panels each year, more than double total global production in 2010.[16]

How did China achieve such a commanding lead in solar panel manufacturing? The US National Renewable Energy Laboratory (NREL) attributes it to a "unique, complex and interdependent" mix of policy, financial, and other factors.[17] One main reason is the enormous scale of Chinese manufacturing. Chinese solar PV factories are usually four times the size of US factories. This allows them to buy materials and equipment at a lower price and take advantage of other economies of scale. In turn, Chinese solar manufacturers have been able to sell their products for about 20 percent less than their competitors.[18]

China is also playing an increasingly important role in driving the technological innovation needed to bring the next generation of solar technologies to market. It has set ambitious solar R&D goals in its 13th Five-Year Plan, and is already beginning to see results. It has restructured its entire government R&D system to strengthen basic research and facilitate the commercialization of innovative technologies. It is working to create technology-innovation hubs throughout the country and staff them with some of the world's best researchers.

Support in China for clean energy is evidenced by the country's investments. China has been the world's top overall investor in clean energy since 2013. It invested a world record $126.6 billion in clean energy in 2017, accounting for 45 percent of the global total.[19] By 2020, there are plans to invest $360 billion more in low-carbon power generation and other clean energy technologies. That number is expected to jump to $6 *trillion* by 2030.[20]

This push to scale up renewable energy has catapulted China to the forefront of a global clean energy revolution, with benefits that extend to every other country, as well as to the climate. The sheer scale of the country's solar panel manufacturing has driven down solar prices faster than anyone had ever imagined. The cost of utility-scale solar PV has plummeted by an astonishing 72 percent since 2009. Onshore wind is also now one of the most competitive sources of new generation capacity. The cost of wind power has dropped by 67 percent since 2009, and wind energy is now the lowest-cost option for new electricity generation in several markets.

Catalyzing the Clean Energy Revolution

China's efforts are not only disrupting its own coal-based energy system, but are also transforming the economics of energy systems worldwide. The plunge in prices has enabled solar and wind to compete head-to-head with coal and other fossil fuels throughout the world. The IEA says that the record-low prices of renewables are now comparable to or even lower than new fossil fuel plants.[21] As a result, the world commissioned a record 157 GW of renewable power projects in 2017, more than the net additions of coal, gas, and nuclear plants combined.[22]

The clean energy revolution is poised to accelerate rapidly. Over the next five years, the IEA anticipates renewable energy to grow by roughly 1,000 GW. This is half of the total capacity of coal-fired power plants worldwide, which took 80 years to build.[23]

Bloomberg New Energy Finance (BNEF), a global research organization that provides independent analysis for corporations, policymakers and other clients, predicts that wind and solar PV plants will dominate the future of electricity, attracting almost three-quarters of the $10.2 trillion the world will invest in new power-generation technologies until 2040. As these clean energy resources continue to crowd out fossil fuels, BNEF expects that only 18 percent of the world's planned new coal plants will ever get built.[24]

In less than a decade, solar energy may be the lowest-cost resource in much of the world. The IEA predicts that solar could become the largest source of energy in the world by 2050. Yet right now solar provides less than 2 percent of the world's – and China's – electricity. Despite its rapid growth, solar energy has a long way to go before it reaches its full potential or plays a significant role in meeting our global climate goals.

A 2016 study by the Massachusetts Institute of Technology and the US NREL estimated that the world is currently on track to install a total of 1,000 GW of cumulative solar power capacity by 2030, up from around 400 GW in 2017. Yet in order to contribute meaningfully to global GHG reductions, we would need between 2,000 and 10,000 GW of solar by that time.[25] Reaching 10,000 GW would require global solar installations to increase about 25 percent every year between now and 2030. It would also require approximately $817 billion in investment in new solar manufacturing capacity.[26]

Trade disputes

The nearly 200 countries that joined the Paris Agreement have a shared interest in accelerating the momentum of solar energy. Yet several countries are slowing down progress, using trade measures to raise the cost of solar energy to protect their domestic manufacturers from lower-priced imports. These measures are often shortsighted and counterproductive.

In January 2018, for example, President Trump imposed a 30 percent tariff on imported solar cells and modules, which are used in 80 percent of US solar installations. This "sun tax" came at the request of two now-bankrupt solar manufacturers, Suniva and SolarWorld Americas. This tariff, however, was widely opposed by the rest of the solar industry because the damage it will cause vastly outweighs any potential benefits. Higher-priced panels will significantly reduce the pace of new solar energy installations, increase climate change emissions, and lead to significant job losses nationwide.

In the United States, the cost of generating power from new solar projects has fallen by more than 85 percent since 2009. Led by these falling prices, solar energy has boomed, growing by an average of 68 percent each year. As a result, solar energy has become one of America's fastest growing industries. In 2016, more than 350,000 people worked in part or in whole on solar energy production, with more than 260,000 of those employees spending most of their time on solar.[27] This is over 40 percent of the overall electrical generation workforce and exceeds the *combined* employment of coal, gas, and oil workers connected with producing electricity, which totaled just under 200,000.[28]

But most of America's solar jobs are in solar panel sales, installation, operation, and maintenance, all of which are now at risk. By slowing demand for solar energy, the tariffs will eliminate an estimated 23,000 jobs in the first year alone.[29] This includes solar panel installation, the fastest-growing employment sector in America – a $40,000-a-year job occupation that had been projected to grow 105 percent between 2016 and 2026.[30]

Trump's "sun tax" is not likely to lead to a renaissance in US manufacturing of solar cells and panels. South Korea, Taiwan, China, and the European Union have already filed challenges to these tariffs with the WTO. Even if they survive, similar "safeguard" tariffs on other industries have failed to achieve sustained US competitiveness after the safeguards terminated.[31]

When the United States imposed anti-dumping and countervailing duty tariffs on solar products from China and Taiwan in 2012 and 2014, respectively, they did not lead to a rebound in US manufacturing. Instead, they pushed Chinese manufacturers to consolidate, vertically integrate, and develop more cost-effective business models, thus becoming even more competitive. They also led the Chinese government to impose its own tariffs on imports of US-made polysilicon, the raw material used in solar cell manufacturing. As a result, US production plummeted, while China dramatically ramped up its own manufacturing capacity. China now produces more than half of the world's polysilicon.[32]

The United States is not the only country to take action intended to protect domestic industries against lower-cost solar imports. The European Union and India have already taken or are considering similar measures. But even if they result in modest gains, these measures are unlikely to enable these countries to compete effectively with China's solar juggernaut. In the meantime, they could slow down attempts to meet their own renewable energy goals.

Integrating renewables into China's domestic market

The number of world records captured by China in renewable energy keeps adding up as the country pushes forward with plans to decarbonize its economy. Yet China faces daunting challenges as it works to integrate wind and solar power into an electricity system and an economy that were built on coal. Overcoming these obstacles will require major structural and policy reforms.

The main problem is that, in large part due to competition between coal and renewables, a large percentage of China's renewable energy is currently being wasted. In 2016, 17 percent of the country's wind energy and 10 percent of its solar energy were "curtailed." This means that wind and solar energy production had to shut down because the grid could not absorb the power, it could not be stored, or other types of energy like coal were given priority. Curtailment rates in some northern and western provinces were alarmingly high, sometimes approaching or exceeding 40 percent. The total amount of wind wasted in China in 2016 would have been enough to power the annual residential electricity use of almost 90 million Chinese residents, about 6.5 percent of the population.

China's leaders understand that tackling renewable energy curtailment is essential to achieve President Xi Jinping's "clean energy revolution," bring back blue skies, and lead the world away from fossil fuels. Curtailment also presents a major challenge for China in meeting its Paris pledges to peak carbon emissions, lower carbon intensity, and increase the share of non-fossil energy sources in its energy mix. On the global level, scaling up renewable energy to the levels needed to combat climate change worldwide will be difficult unless China manages to connect most, if not virtually all, of its renewable energy to the grid.

The 13th Five-Year Plan sets a goal of reducing curtailment to no more than 5 percent by 2020. It also sets targets for how much renewable energy is actually generated, rather than simply how much capacity is built. But to reach these targets, China must address several fundamental obstacles.

Regional imbalance

One reason why so much clean energy is wasted is a geographic mismatch between where renewable energy is generated and where it is needed. More than 70 percent of China's large wind and solar plants are in remote regions where there is little demand, far from the populated industrial regions in the east. The development of long-distance transmission lines, however, has not kept up with the surge of new generation capacity.

One reason for this is that China's transmission line plans are running into resistance from provincial and local governments. Local officials, who are not eager to buy energy from other provinces, often engage in protectionist behavior on behalf of their own coal and renewable generators. This hampers the development of regional and interprovincial markets that would facilitate the integration of renewable energy.[33]

China is halfway through a plan to spend $88 billion on a massive ultra-high voltage (UHV) transmission network, with 16 new UHV lines to be brought online by 2020.[34] One of these planned lines will connect the far-flung provinces of Xinjiang in the west and Anhui in the east, and, at 3,324 kilometers long, will be the longest UHV line in the world.[35] The central government has urged the country's northern and western provinces to prioritize transmission of renewable energy resources above coal. Yet there is currently no regulatory framework in place to ensure that this happens, and transmission rules still favor coal.

China is also working to shift investment in new renewables away from regions with high curtailment toward provinces where the demand is greatest. The NEA, for example, has launched investment risk alert systems for new wind and utility-scale solar projects, similar to the risk alert system for coal plants. The provinces of Gansu, Jilin, and Xinjiang received red warnings in 2018 and will not be allowed to approve and/or connect new wind projects unless and until they can reduce curtailment significantly.

In addition, China is pushing for greater development of small and medium-sized projects, known as distributed generation, that can be installed in any part of the country near electricity users. Nearly one-third of the new solar capacity installed in 2017 fell into this category, ranging from poverty alleviation projects in rural areas to rooftop solar in mammoth industrial parks.[36]

Grid inflexibility

Another major reason for the large amount of wasted renewable energy is the lack of flexibility in China's electricity grid. Like those of many other countries, the grid was originally designed for constant, centralized power production. Renewable energy, in contrast, is intermittent – fluctuating according to weather conditions, time of day, even air pollution levels, which can reduce the amount of solar penetration.

In most countries, power grid operators determine which generating plants to operate (or "dispatch") multiple times a day to meet constantly shifting demand in a way that minimizes short-term costs.

This approach rewards renewable energy resources, because, unlike coal plants, their fuel (the wind and the sun) is free.

China's power sector, however, was designed decades ago to support its rapid industrialization by making it attractive to build coal-fired power plants. That design is still largely in place today. China still guarantees coal plants a set number of operating hours each year, and compensates them at a fixed rate per kWh, regardless of the availability of cheaper and cleaner alternatives. This approach worked well at a time when coal accounted for 80 percent of China's electric generation, but it is too inflexible to suit current needs.

In the September 2015 US–China Joint Statement on climate change, President Xi Jinping pledged that China "will promote green power dispatch, giving priority, in distribution and dispatching, to renewable power generation and fossil fuel power generation of higher efficiency and lower emission levels."[37] Since then, China has been working to develop a green dispatch system as part of a major power sector reform effort. The aim of these reforms is to improve reliability, increase the use of market mechanisms, save energy, reduce emissions, and increase the use of renewables and distributed generation.

Catalyzing the Clean Energy Revolution

Chinese NGOs are stepping in to help. In 2016, Friends of Nature (FON), one of the country's oldest environmental NGOs, brought separate lawsuits against two utility companies in Ningxia and Gansu provinces, which suffer some of the worst curtailment rates in China. The lawsuits seek damages ($49 million in one case) against the utilities for failure to compensate renewable energy generators for curtailed wind and solar electricity, as required by China's Renewable Energy Law. FON hopes that if grid operators are required to pay for the generation of renewables even when it is curtailed, they will work harder to integrate it into the grid, further reducing the power sector's reliance on coal. At the time of writing, both lawsuits are in the pre-trial phase.

China's reform efforts are showing signs of progress, but overhauling the world's largest power sector to remove coal's built-in advantages is no easy task. Despite these challenges, efforts to reduce renewable energy curtailment have begun to yield results. In 2017, China reduced its national curtailment rate by 5 percent for wind and 4.3 percent for solar PV, according to official statistics; Gansu and Xinjiang reported improvements of more than 10 percent; and several provinces are expected to eliminate curtailments altogether in the near future.

Pushing forward with the power sector reforms described above will be essential for China to fully address the problem of curtailment and reap all the benefits of its world record renewable energy drive.

One of the most innovative ideas for improving renewable energy integration is to coordinate electric vehicle charging with the availability of renewable energy on the grid.[38] It may be difficult to fathom how charging electric vehicles could have any impact on curtailment. That is, until you understand how fast the electric vehicle industry is growing in China.

4

Jumpstarting the Electric Vehicle Industry

In 2002, I met an automotive engineer named Wan Gang, who had just returned to his native Shanghai from Germany to head up the Center of Automotive Engineering at Tongji University. China was just beginning its love affair with the automobile, and sales and production of gasoline-fueled passenger vehicles were growing dramatically. But Wan Gang had a different vision. At his urging, the Chinese government set up a national research program designed to leapfrog over the internal combustion engine and develop cleaner alternatives. The program aimed to commercialize battery electric vehicles (EVs), achieve large-scale production of hybrid vehicles, and develop fuel cell vehicle (FCV) prototypes.

With funding from the program, Wan Gang established a Clean Vehicles Technology Center at the university, focused on fuel cell research and development. My organization, NRDC, collaborated with Wan Gang to raise awareness in China about the challenges and opportunities of commercializing FCVs. His center partnered with the Pan Asia Automotive Technology Center, a joint venture of General Motors and the Shanghai Automotive Industry Corporation. Together, they developed China's first fuel cell concept car, which I was invited to test drive. I remember thinking that China was on the cusp of a clean vehicle revolution.

That revolution is now in full swing, thanks to the vision and abilities of Wan Gang. Within five years of his return to China, he moved to Beijing to become Minister of Science and Technology (a position he held until March 2018). Under Wan Gang's leadership, China's enormous bet on what it calls new energy vehicles (NEVs) – including battery electric, plug-in hybrids and FCVs – has transformed the landscape of the global automotive industry, with major implications for the battle against climate change.

China has compelling reasons to back the development of EVs and other NEVs. Switching to EVs helps clear the air in China's cities and eases the country's record-high dependence on foreign oil. (China's dependency on foreign oil reached

67 percent in 2017, as it surpassed the United States in oil imports; US dependency on foreign oil, on the other hand, fell to 19 percent in 2017, as domestic production continued to grow.)[1] As more renewable energy is integrated into the grid, EVs will reduce overall CO_2 emissions and accelerate China's transition to a low-carbon economy. Developing the capacity to produce EVs and batteries also helps China to compete in the twenty-first century as electrification, automation, and decarbonization technologies are changing the automobile market.

China first targeted NEVs for development in its 10th Five-Year Plan (2001–05) and began offering subsidies and other support measures in the early 2000s. In 2010, NEVs were designated as a strategic emerging industry, along with solar and wind power. The government committed $15 billion over 10 years for the country's leading auto and battery companies to create an electric car industry, starting in 20 pilot cities. In 2012, the State Council called for the production and sale of at least 500,000 electric and hybrid vehicles by 2015.

US journalist Thomas Friedman realized in 2010 that China was positioning itself for global leadership in the electric vehicle industry. He called it a "moon shot," a "big, multibillion-dollar,

25-year-horizon, game-changing investment."[2] Friedman called upon the United States to cooperate with China in what would be a win-win collaboration for both countries. With support from Wan Gang, the two countries did establish a bilateral Clean Energy Research Center (CERC) in 2009 to facilitate joint research and development on clean vehicle technologies by teams of scientists and engineers from both countries.

Yet, for many years, China's fledgling EV industry suffered from many of the same challenges being faced in other countries. Consumers were reluctant to buy EVs because of their high expense, inadequate range, and limited charging infrastructure. Low demand made it difficult to justify scaling up production levels or investing in infrastructure. By the end of 2013, China's State Grid Company had built only 400 charging stations, compared with more than 20,000 in the United States. China's domestic automotive industry lacked the capacity to develop cutting-edge NEV technologies. Yet, at the same time, trade barriers prevented foreign automakers from producing or selling NEVs in China.[3]

By the end of 2013, after more than a decade of effort, China was nowhere near meeting its 2015 target. Fewer than 18,000 of the nearly 22 million vehicles sold in China in 2013 were NEVs, representing less than 0.1 percent of all auto sales. In contrast, the United States sold 96,000 NEVs that year, largely driven by California's Zero Emission Vehicle (ZEV) program.[4]

Then, perhaps in response to mounting concerns about the 2013 "airpocalypse," China launched its "moon shot" in earnest. In September 2013, the same month that China released its Air Pollution Prevention and Control Action Plan, four central government ministries established a national program to provide NEV purchase subsidies of up to $9,700 per vehicle. These were the most generous purchase subsidies of any country except for Norway. In 2014, the State Council exempted domestic NEVs from a 10 percent purchase tax. Local governments began to offer additional purchase subsidies, often as large as those offered by the central government, resulting in some cases of total subsidies of more than $16,000 per vehicle.

China expects to pay a massive $60.7 billion in NEV subsidies between 2015 and 2020.[5] After 2020, it plans to gradually phase out the national subsidy program and eliminate local subsidies, which local governments often used to protect NEV manufacturers within their borders.[6] In the meantime, the national program has been revamped to provide larger subsidies to advanced NEVs with longer range and battery energy densities, and reduce or eliminate subsidies for lower range models.

The market for NEVs is expected to accelerate further, even without subsidies, due to falling battery prices and a range of other supportive government policies. Other countries such as Norway are also considering reducing their EV subsidies. The United States offers buyers a $7,500 tax credit, which is phased out for EVs from automakers that have sold a total of 200,000 or more. This puts companies like General Motors and Tesla at a competitive disadvantage, especially compared to foreign companies that are just beginning to sell EVs in the United States.

In the meantime, EVs are getting a boost in China from public transit, fleet sales, and car sharing services, which are more climate-friendly than passenger cars in any case. Shenzhen, Taiyuan, and other cities have switched all their buses to electric. Beijing is replacing all 69,000 of its taxis with EVs. Didi Chuxing, the leading ride-hailing service in China, plans to invest over $150 million, build a countrywide charging network, and expand its fleet of EVs, already the world's largest, to 1 million by 2020.[7]

Some cities offer nonmonetary benefits to individual NEV buyers, which in many cases are even more attractive than subsidies. Some provide free license plates to NEV owners, enabling them to avoid having to pay hefty fees or wait months or years for a license plate. Seven out of ten NEVs are sold in just six Chinese cities that restrict license plates for conventional fuel vehicles.[8] Other cities offer NEV drivers access to bus lanes, exemptions from peak traffic restrictions, free charging, and free parking.

In 2015, China named NEVs as one of ten priority sectors in its ambitious Made in China 2025 industrial initiative. The goal of this initiative is to comprehensively upgrade China's industry to make it more innovative and competitive, to localize production of components and final products, and to move Chinese firms up the global value-added chain. China intends to identify a few of the more than 80 existing NEV companies as national champions, helping them to develop into top global brands by 2025 and dominate the EV market by 2030. The plan also calls for key systems, including power batteries and electric motors, to reach world-leading levels by 2020 and achieve 80 percent of global market share by 2025. It should be noted, however, that while accelerating global EV market penetration would benefit consumers, the environment, and the climate, market domination by any one country to the exclusion of other competitors could hinder that effort.

China took another game-changing step in 2017, when it decided to leverage its position as the world's largest auto market to jumpstart the demand for EVs. In September of that year, the government announced that it was developing a timetable to completely ban the manufacture and sale of fossil fuel-powered vehicles in China. Some predict that the ban might come into force as early as 2030.

This move, coming from the world's largest vehicle market, adds critical momentum to the emerging international movement to phase out the use of internal combustion engine (ICE) vehicles. Other countries that have announced plans to ban the sale of ICE vehicles include the Netherlands, India, Scotland, the United Kingdom, and France. Germany is debating a ban, and Norway plans to reach 100 percent EVs by 2025 through an aggressive tax scheme.

California, the long-time leader in US clean vehicle efforts, is also considering a ban on gasoline-powered vehicles in the state by 2040. The move would help California achieve its goal to cut GHG emissions by 80 percent between 1990 and 2050. If the ban is approved, the state's motor vehicles department would only register vehicles that have zero carbon dioxide emissions.

While China's call to phase out the sale of conventional petrol vehicles is an important signal to industry and other world leaders, the country's NEV mandate policy, which went into effect in April 2018, has triggered a major paradigm shift in the global auto industry. This policy, a modified version of California's ZEV program, requires large auto manufacturers to obtain NEV credits equivalent to 10 percent of their conventional vehicle production in 2019, and 12 percent in 2020. Manufacturers can receive up to six credits per vehicle for those that utilize more advanced technology. Carmakers that fail to produce or import enough NEVs to meet these targets must buy credits from other automakers or pay fines.[9]

China also imposed strict new fuel economy standards, comparable to those in Europe, that will also drive EV production. To achieve compliance with both the NEV mandate and the new fuel economy standards, experts estimate that automakers will need to ensure that 7 to 8 percent of their car sales will be electric-powered by 2020.[10] This is a major increase, since NEVs accounted for only 2 percent of total car sales in China in 2017.

The impact on the global automobile industry has been seismic, as foreign automakers speed up their efforts to develop EVs to avoid being left behind. Volkswagen AG, the world's largest automaker, plans to invest nearly $12 billion in EV development and launch five NEV models a year in China through 2025. Ford announced plans for at least 15 new electric-powered models and a new $756 million plant in China. General Motors plans to have at least ten all-electric or hybrid models on the Chinese market by 2020. Daimler is investing around $750 million in a Chinese battery plant to power electric Mercedes-Benz cars. Volvo announced that all its new models will include electric drive by 2019. The list goes on and on.

To meet the NEV mandate, many foreign automakers have developed joint ventures with Chinese companies. Tesla, counting on its brand cachet, reportedly plans instead to build a wholly owned EV factory in Shanghai's free trade zone. Not having to form a joint venture will allow Tesla to protect its technology and keep all the profits, but its cars will not be eligible for subsidies and will be subject to a 25 percent import tariff. This situation may change, however, as China announced in April 2018 that it will lower import tariffs for automobiles and phase out rules requiring foreign

NEV manufacturers to share factory ownership and profits with Chinese companies.

Virtually all foreign manufacturers, except for Tesla, have complained about not having fair access to China's EV market, since the rules favor Chinese automakers and battery producers. But these same automakers have long resisted California and US government regulations designed to catalyze EV development in the United States, once the world's largest market.[11] They have successfully lobbied the Trump Administration to propose weakening the Corporate Average Fuel Economy (CAFE) standards to allow them to sell more SUVs and pickup trucks, which yield higher profits, and fewer high-efficiency or electric vehicles.

These automakers failed to capitalize on their enormous technological advantages to help create and dominate the market for EVs. This led China to identify this technology as one that was "bypassed" by foreign automakers, which are now struggling to catch up.[12]

China's "moon shot" is paying off. China overtook the United States in 2015 as having the world's largest electric car market. In 2017, more than 605,000 passenger NEVs were sold in China, nearly half the world's total. China also sold 198,000 commercial NEVs, mostly electric buses. China is now home to about 99 percent of the world's 385,000 electric buses; every five weeks, its cities convert the equivalent of London's entire working fleet.[13]

Total NEV sales in 2017 were four times higher than in the United States, the second largest market.[14] Of the sales in China itself, 90 percent were by Chinese automakers. BYD, the Shenzhen-based cellphone battery maker turned electric car manufacturer with financing from Warren Buffett and Samsung, is now the world's largest EV manufacturer, capturing 30 percent of the Chinese market; the company also operates North America's largest electric bus manufacturing facility north of Los Angeles, with more than 700 employees.[15]

China now has more than 1.2 million NEVs on the road, half the world's total. It expects to sell another 1 million in 2018, even before the NEV mandate program comes into effect. The country hopes to put 5 million NEVs on the road by 2020, about one-quarter of its current annual total vehicle sales, and 7 million by 2025. At this rate, these targets are likely to be reached or even exceeded.

The main obstacles are still the high cost and limited range of EV batteries. The world's automakers are feverishly competing with one another to develop a reliable, long-lasting, inexpensive EV battery, perhaps the biggest obstacle standing in the way of competitiveness in the EV market. As my colleague put it: "Whoever wins has the chance to become the pioneering, market-dominating Henry Ford of the next automotive era."[16]

China wants to be that pioneer. The country is now home to about two-thirds of global lithium-ion battery production, compared with 10 percent in the United States.[17] It is also building about half of the 20 or more battery mega-factories now under construction.[18] There are currently more than 140 EV battery manufacturers in China, but one stands out.[19] Contemporary Amperex Technology Ltd., or CATL, is on track to beat Tesla to become the world's largest EV battery cell manufacturer, with a $2 billion expansion that could begin operations as early as 2020.[20]

As is the case with solar panels, the scale of China's EV battery manufacturing is bringing down prices throughout the world. After beginning to mass produce its first-generation battery system in 2013, China has already reduced the cost by two-thirds.[21] The costs of a lithium-ion battery pack are expected to drop below $100 per kWh over the next decade.[22] BNEF forecasts that falling battery costs will make EVs cost-competitive with conventional vehicles within eight to ten years. BNEF expects that more than half of new car sales worldwide –

and therefore a third of the global light-duty vehicle fleet – will be electric-powered by 2040. Such a fleet (totaling 530 million EVs) will need 8 million fewer barrels of transportation fuel per day – roughly one-twelfth of today's global production.[23] The impact on global CO_2 emissions would be enormous.

Even China's National Petroleum Corporation forecasts that China's oil consumption will peak by 2030 and gasoline consumption by 2025. China's EV policies and future ban on gasoline-powered vehicles can, if fully implemented, help it to achieve peak oil production even earlier.

Challenges

In addition to the high cost and limited range of EV batteries, China faces another key challenge – making its charging network more widely available, accessible, and convenient to use. There are now 480,000 EV charging points in China, including 210,000 publicly accessible units. But these are only used, on average, 15 percent of the time. The reasons include a mismatch between where EV charging stations are located and where they are needed most, and low technical standards that make charging difficult. The central government plans included an additional 600,000 charging stations nationwide in 2018. It has also urged local governments to begin subsidizing the construction of charging facilities rather than NEV purchases.

The growing number of NEVs could put a strain on China's electric grid, but with smart charging and demand response (DR), EVs could play an essential role in helping to integrate renewables. My organization, NRDC, has tested the potential for EVs to take part in DR programs in China.[24] The idea is for electric utilities to improve renewable energy integration by coordinating EV charging with conditions on the grid.[25]

EVs constitute an ideal technology for utilities to work with for two reasons. First, they can store a lot of energy, which means that if they are charged when surplus renewable energy is available (such as during the night when wind power is abundant but energy demand is low), then they can hold on to that energy for later use; second, they usually have some flexibility regarding the time when they are charged, so DR providers can adjust their charging times in order to match electricity demand with fluctuations in energy supply.

A February 2018 report by NRDC, China's Energy Research Institute, and the Energy Storage Alliance estimates that there will be more than 100 million EVs in China by 2030. If China's wind and solar power installed capacities each reach 1 terawatt (TW) by 2030, the report estimates that vehicle-to-grid storage technology will be able to store 13 consecutive hours of flexible power. This will play a key role in balancing the power grid system when there is a high proportion of renewable energy in the mix.[26]

In addition, as China promotes the use of distributed renewable power generation, it needs to find ways to integrate NEV deployment with charging stations powered directly by renewable energy. Ramping up renewable energy, in turn, will help to ensure that NEVs are indeed a cleaner alternative to fossil fuel-powered cars.

Some experts are concerned that China's massive scale-up of conventional EV technology will crowd out the next generation of technologies. Recognizing this concern, China has set targets for battery manufacturers to catch up with more advanced Japanese battery technology, including more than doubling traveling distance and energy density. China has also extended its subsidy program to reward EVs with more advanced battery technologies, such as nickel, manganese, and cobalt batteries. In addition, as part of the US–China CERC Clean Vehicles Consortium, Chinese and American researchers are working together to explore advanced battery and vehicle technologies.

EVs are only one facet of China's low-carbon urbanization drive. Much more still needs to be done to reduce the reliance on passenger cars, scale up public transit, and design more sustainable and walkable cities. China also needs to address the life-cycle environmental impacts of the batteries used in electrical vehicles, from the mining of raw materials to battery recycling and disposal. In March 2018, the government announced plans to start an EV battery recycling program in four regions.

The *Wall Street Journal* reported that China has created the world's largest EV market by "sheer force of will."[27] In doing so, it has enabled a key technology in the battle against climate change to begin to take off globally. Yet despite the explosive growth, EVs currently form only a tiny share of the global auto industry, accounting for no more than 0.2 percent of the total number of passenger light duty vehicles. Like solar and wind power, EVs need to scale up significantly before they can make a real contribution to fighting climate change. In order for this to happen, China's financial system – and that of the entire world – must go green.

5

Greening China's Financial System

A few years ago, while living in Hong Kong, I met an economist named Ma Jun (not the environmental advocate with the same name). As chief China economist at Deutsche Bank AG, Ma Jun spoke passionately about the economics of pollution, explaining why addressing environmental challenges does not have to jeopardize economic growth. Instead, he argued that strong environmental measures could be a powerful catalyst for transforming China's economic structure to achieve long-term sustainable growth.

In 2014, Ma Jun was invited to return to Beijing to become chief economist of the research bureau at the People's Bank of China. Since that time, I have watched with growing interest as he has become a global leader in green finance, turning his innovative ideas into action, not just in China, but throughout the world.

Greening China's Financial System

Ma Jun estimates that China needs 4 trillion RMB ($636 billion) a year for environmental remediation, clean energy, energy efficiency, green buildings, and clean transportation. But public financing can only provide 15 percent of the amount needed. He says that a system of green finance – one that provides incentives for green investments while restricting polluting investments – can mobilize private capital to provide the rest.

As chairman of the Green Finance Committee of the China Society for Finance and Banking, Ma Jun has spearheaded a package of reforms designed to green China's financial system and stimulate investments to further its climate and sustainable development objectives. Among other things, he led the drafting of China's 2016 Green Finance Guidelines, the world's first comprehensive framework for green finance.[1] The guidelines provide the basis for a complete green finance system, including expanding green credit, developing a green bond market, and establishing green development funds. They also cover green stock indices, green insurance, green guarantee programs, environmental risk disclosure systems, and carbon finance.[2]

Green bonds

In 2016, Ma Jun played a key role in launching China's green bond market. Green bonds are similar to regular bonds, except that the proceeds must be used for projects with environmental and/or climate benefits. By the end of its first year, $36.9 billion worth of green bonds had been issued in China, nearly 40 percent of the world total.[3] As with markets for solar panels and electric vehicles, China's efforts are accelerating the growth of the green bond market worldwide.

Although pleased with this progress, Ma Jun noted that green bonds only actually constitute 2 percent of China's total bond market, whereas 20 percent of investment in China needs to be green to meet the country's ambitious environmental and climate targets.[4] China is looking to international investors to help close the gap. But not all projects that are currently eligible for the country's green bonds are attractive to international investors. To support China's war on air pollution, for example, some coal plant retrofit projects designed to reduce conventional pollutants are eligible for green bonds, even if they do nothing to reduce carbon emissions.[5] Ma Jun's Green Finance Committee is working to harmonize local green bond standards with those of international markets.

China issued another $37.1 billion in green bonds in 2017, up 4.5 percent from the previous year. Sixty-two percent, or $22.9 billion, of those green bonds were aligned with international green bond standards. This amounts to 15 percent of the world's green bond issuance, making China the second largest green bond market in the world after the United States.[6]

The G20

In 2016, China assumed the rotating presidency of the G20, which brings together leaders of the 20 largest industrialized and emerging economies. In preparation for the annual G20 summit, which was held in Hangzhou, China established a G20 Green Finance Study Group (GFSG) with more than 80 participants from every G20 country. The GFSG was co-chaired by Ma Jun, representing China, and Mark Carney, Governor of the Bank of England, representing the UK. This was the first time that green finance gained a spot on the G20 agenda.

As GFSG co-chair, Ma Jun played a leading role in forging an international consensus on green finance. The GFSG prepared a synthesis report that explains the importance of green finance in sustainable development, explores challenges for increasing green financial flows, and lays out seven policy recommendations for countries to create enabling environments for green finance.[7] The G20 leaders approved the report in their annual communiqué, recognizing, for the first time, the importance of greening the world's financial system.[8]

The United States and China also used the G20 as an opportunity to release peer reviews of the details of fossil fuel subsidies issued in each country, the first G20 countries to do so.[9] The US review calculated that the country issued over $8 billion in inefficient fossil fuel subsidies, while the subsidies issued in China were valued at $14.5 billion. While it is important to recognize these reviews as a step toward greater international transparency on fossil fuel subsidies, the next step is getting an internationally agreed deadline for phasing out inefficient subsidies, bolstered by inventories and a peer review system to help remove the bias in the financial system in favor of fossil fuels.

The G20 also faces the challenge of putting its recommendations for greening the financial system into action abroad, especially since public financing from G20 governments for overseas coal projects reached a five-year high in 2017. This financing, driven primarily by China, Japan, India, and Korea, totaled at least $13 billion in 2017, far outweighing public financing of overseas renewable energy projects.[10]

In September 2017, Ma Jun was appointed UN Environment's Special Advisor on Sustainable Finance. According to the head of UN Environment, Dr. Ma's role will be "not only to help turn existing thinking into action, but to dream up new and daring initiatives to increase the flow of public and private capital toward sustainability."[11] Ma Jun continues to serve as chairman of China's Green Finance Committee, where, among other responsibilities, he is working to green China's Belt and Road initiative (BRI).

BRI

The Belt and Road Initiative, President Xi Jinping's signature global strategy, is a regional economic and development initiative that aims to strengthen global infrastructure, expand trade, and build international logistics gateways. Launched in 2013, BRI now covers 70 countries in four continents and includes over two-thirds of the global population. At an estimated cumulative investment of between $4 and $8 trillion,[12] BRI may become the largest infrastructure project in history, dwarfing the United States' $130 billion (perhaps $1.4 trillion in today's dollars) Marshall Plan, which rebuilt Europe after World War II.[13]

The countries in the BRI play a critical role in global climate efforts. Together (including China), they account for over half of global energy consumption and 60 percent of global CO_2 emissions.[14] Most face major challenges in providing access to electricity and modernizing their energy infrastructure. Many require assistance to implement their Paris climate pledges. Thus, there is a large opportunity, as well as a pressing need, for China to cooperate with BRI countries to accelerate the use of clean energy and low-carbon technologies.

Some fear that, as China greens its domestic economy, Chinese companies in energy-intensive sectors will increasingly seek to export their capital and technology overseas to BRI countries lacking strong environmental governance. According to one database, 66 percent of power sector lending from China's two global policy banks between 2000 and 2016 went to coal projects.[15] A recent study by China's Global Environmental Institute (GEI) found that from 2001 through 2016, China participated in 240 coal-fired power projects with a total installed capacity of 251 GW in 25 BRI countries.[16] Were China to continue to invest heavily in fossil fuels in BRI countries, it could lock in high emissions for decades to come, impeding global efforts to achieve the Paris Agreement's 2 degree and 1.5 degree Celsius climate targets.

Ma Jun acknowledges this risk, saying that emissions in BRI countries could reach three times those in China if nothing is done to green the initiative. He says his mission is to "make sure Chinese investors are seeking green investments in the belt and road region."[17]

As one of the countries that is most vulnerable to the impacts of climate change, China recognizes that it is in its own interest to reduce emissions both at home and abroad. At a May 2017 Belt and Road Forum attended by 30 world leaders, President Xi called for a "new vision of green development and a way of life and work that is green, low-carbon, circular and sustainable."[18]

The Joint Communiqué released after the Forum expressed a determination to take "urgent action on climate change" and to manage "natural resources in an equitable and sustainable manner." It further emphasized the "importance of economic, social, fiscal, financial and environmental sustainability of projects, and of promoting high environmental standards."[19] Following the Forum, four of China's ministries jointly issued a document entitled *Guidance on Promoting Green Belt and Road,* which calls for incorporating eco-environmental protection into all aspects of the BRI.[20]

On September 5, 2017, Ma Jun's Green Finance Committee, along with several government agencies, released *Environmental Risk Management Initiative for China's Overseas Investment*. The document sets out certain principles that Chinese investors should strive to uphold. It urges investors engaged in overseas investment to fully understand and comply with the environmental laws and regulations of host countries, as well as relevant international standards. It specifically directs institutional investors to refer to the UN Principles for Responsible Investment. It encourages them to consider environmental, social, and governance (ESG) factors in evaluating investments, and emphasizes the importance of disclosing ESG information.

The document is not legally binding, but, by some accounts, the government is in the process of drafting legally binding rules on overseas investment, "including specific plans for implementing each article of the initiative to form a detailed operational guide."[21] Implementation will be crucial to the success of this effort.

There are some positive trends. China's outbound investment in the renewables sector is increasing. In 2017, 18 large (i.e., exceeding US$1 billion) overseas deals were made for renewables, new energy, and network investment, for a total of $44 billion. This compares to $32 billion in 2016, which was itself a record year. China's outbound investment in renewables to date has mainly targeted developed countries. But China exported $8 billion of solar equipment to BRI countries in 2017, helping it to overtake the United States and Germany as the world's top exporter of environmental goods and services.[22] And Chinese institutions have begun to support wind and solar projects in developing countries, such as the Export-Import Bank of China's financing for the 300 MW Cauchari Solar Complex in Argentina, which will be Latin America's largest solar park.[23]

The BRI is also expanding China's green bond market. A number of major banks, including the China Development Bank, ICBC, and the Bank of China have already issued green bonds to support green infrastructure in BRI countries. In 2017, for example, the ICBC issued a $2.15 billion Certified Climate Bond that included a BRI tranche – the biggest single tranche in euro-denominated green bonds by a Chinese issuer.[24] Bond proceeds will be used for eligible projects in renewable energy, low-carbon transportation, energy efficiency, and sustainable water. In November 2017, the China

Development Bank issued its first-ever international green bond, raising $500 million and €1 billion in funding to support green projects in Kazakhstan, Pakistan, and Sri Lanka, among others.[25]

China has an enormous opportunity to help BRI countries to reduce CO_2 emissions in a cost-effective manner by sharing its deep expertise in energy efficiency. Energy efficiency is the most important strategy for reaching an economically optimal 2 degree Celsius scenario.[26] China has been responsible for over half of the world's energy conservation progress since the late twentieth century, according to China's special climate envoy Xie Zhenhua.[27] It now ranks sixth in the world in terms of energy efficiency,[28] thanks to strong government commitment, ambitious targets, and effective policies for energy conservation and emission reduction.[29]

Moreover, as the costs of wind and solar power continue to plummet, the IEA forecasts that the growth in renewable generation over the next five years will be twice as large as that of gas and coal combined.[30] China can leverage its position as the global leader in renewable energy to accelerate the growth of clean energy in BRI countries.

According to the International Financial Corporation, $23 trillion in clean energy technology investment is needed between now and 2030 if the world is to meet the Paris climate goals.[31] With the help of Ma Jun, China's innovative leadership in green finance can help to mobilize public and private capital to meet that need.

Epilogue:
China in the Driving Seat

Leadership matters. Under the leadership of President Barack Obama and President Xi Jinping, climate change collaboration flourished as the world's two largest greenhouse gas emitters shared technical, market, and financial expertise. By working constructively together to jointly develop and promote climate solutions, the United States and China strengthened their respective efforts to develop green, low-carbon, and climate-resilient economies. Their leadership also helped to galvanize global climate action that culminated in the Paris Agreement.

This has now been brought to a screeching halt under the Trump Administration. Trump has not only abdicated America's global climate leadership, but is trying to overturn the very programs that were designed to strengthen its leadership role in clean energy. Trump is trying to gut the Clean Power Plan, even as China imposes a host of tough measures to decarbonize its coal-dependent power sector, including a national cap on coal consumption. Trump is trying to roll back America's clean car and fuel standards, even as China rolls out the world's largest New Energy Vehicle mandate. Trump imposed a "sun tax" that is eliminating well-paying jobs in America's fastest growing economic sector, even as China is investing nearly as much money in renewable energy as the rest of the world put together.

As the United States – which created the first solar cell and built the first practical electric vehicle – falls behind, China is vaulting forward. China has identified the most promising clean technologies of the twenty-first century, and is putting its considerable resources in place to support these strategic industries. The country's massive investments have set in motion a dramatic downward spiral in the cost of renewable energy that is reverberating throughout the world, with major benefits for the climate. In 2017, record low auction prices for solar PV were seen in countries from Dubai and Abu Dhabi to Mexico and Chile. In March 2018, India hosted the first summit of the International Solar Alliance, a non-profit treaty-based group of 121 countries promoting the use of solar energy throughout the world.

China's war on coal – and the plummeting price of renewables – are making it increasingly difficult for the coal industry to compete in world energy markets. Coal plant closure momentum is growing in Europe. Two-thirds of existing Indian coal generation is now more expensive than new solar or wind generation. More than 20 countries have joined a global alliance to accelerate the phase-out of traditional coal power. And despite Trump's efforts to prop up the US coal industry, power companies in the United States are preparing to retire almost 12 GW of coal-fired capacity in 2018, about 4 percent of the entire American coal fleet.

China's climate policies have always reflected its own national interest, but now it has redefined its national interest to center around sustainability, innovation, and clean energy. This too is climate leadership. Other developing countries can learn from China's successful efforts to reduce its carbon intensity and decouple economic growth from energy consumption.

It is also in China's own interest to leverage its leadership in green finance in order to shift models of global development toward lower carbon alternatives. The Belt and Road Initiative provides a crucial opportunity, as President Xi said, for China to take a "driving seat" in international efforts to respond to climate change. China can use its BRI platform to accelerate the spread of low-carbon technologies rather than obsolete fossil fuel-based infrastructure, in a way that will support China's own shift to a more stable, higher-quality growth model.

China's push to become a global leader in clean technology brings it substantial economic benefits. The trade barriers erected by the Trump Administration and some other countries in response, however, are not in anyone's economic interest. In a comprehensive 2017 report, *The New Solar System*, a group of Stanford University researchers laid out a detailed strategy for accelerating the growth of the global solar industry. They argue persuasively that the best way for any country to derive lasting economic gain from the solar industry is to help maximize the industry's efficient global growth. They urge the United States and China to focus on leveraging their own comparative advantages and pursue technological innovation rather than trying to beat each other. The report also explains why clear government policies and support for solar R&D and solar deployment, rather than tariffs, are the most effective drivers of solar manufacturing.[1]

The same approach applies to electric vehicles. China's announcement that it will lower import tariffs for automobiles and phase out rules requiring foreign NEV manufacturers to share factory ownership and profits with Chinese companies is a welcome move.

Despite the rapid progress of the global clean energy revolution, China and other countries face many of the same formidable challenges. It is therefore in every country's self-interest to share experience and insights on how to address these challenges. What is the best way to help displaced coal industry workers learn new skills and find new jobs to support their families? How can we reform the institutions and industries standing in the way of a high-renewables, low-cost, reliable grid? What are the most innovative solutions to redefine mobility and create more sustainable and climate-resilient cities?

Time is running out. UN Secretary-General António Guterres says the window of opportunity to meet the 2 degree Celsius target could close in 20 years or less, and we may only have five years to bend the emissions curve towards 1.5 degrees. Every country must strengthen its own climate ambitions and work together to accelerate and scale up solutions.

Epilogue: China in the Driving Seat

My colleague Yang Fuqiang, one of China's leading experts on climate and clean energy, estimates that for China to do its part in keeping the rise in global average temperature to well below 2 degrees Celsius, it must continue to drive and intensify its decarbonization efforts. Coal consumption must stay below its 2013 peak, reaching no more than 0.91 tons of coal equivalent by 2050, accounting for 16.7 percent of the total energy mix. Oil consumption must peak by 2030, and total energy consumption by 2040. This would correspond to total CO_2 emissions of about 5.5 billion tons by 2050. These estimates assume that China reaches a post-industrialization state by 2020, and that by 2050, China's GDP growth rate declines to 2.6 percent; its population is about 1.43 billion, with three-quarters residing in urban areas; energy efficiency improves by 300 percent from 2015 levels; and the country implements strong environmental protection and air pollution reduction measures.

The good news is that China is deeply committed to achieving its low-carbon transition, and has already made major progress. As a result, although China is still the world's largest GHG emitter, it is arguably doing more today than any other country to reduce global carbon emissions – though it continues to face enormous challenges. But China cannot save the planet on its own. There is plenty of room – and need – for all countries to accelerate their efforts, collaborate, and even engage in healthy competition in the battle against climate change. States, provinces, cities, businesses, investors, and individuals throughout the world are also stepping up their efforts to meet our shared global objectives. The challenges ahead require nothing less.

Further Reading

For those wishing to learn more about the drivers of global climate change, clean energy solutions, and the obstacles to progress, Joseph Romm's book, *Climate Change: What Everyone Needs to Know* (2nd ed., Oxford University Press, 2018) is a comprehensive and highly accessible primer. Several recent documentaries provide vivid first-hand accounts of the devastating impacts of climate change around the world and what experts say can be done about them. These include Leonardo DiCaprio's *Before the Flood* (National Geographic, 2017) and Al Gore's *An Inconvenient Sequel: Truth to Power* (Paramount Pictures, 2017). The Emmy-winning climate change series, *Years of Living Dangerously* (National Geographic, 2014/2017) includes an episode on China's efforts to reduce emissions even as its economy continues to grow (http://yearsofliv

ingdangerously.com/story/elephant-in-the-room/). NRDC's website (https://www.nrdc.org/issues/climate-change) includes up-to-date information on what citizens can do to help fight climate change.

Elizabeth Economy conducted seminal research on the roots and evolution of China's climate diplomacy, as discussed in Chapter 1. Her work can be found, among other places, in *The Making of Chinese Foreign and Security Policy in the Era of Reform, 1978–2000* (Stanford University Press, 2001). More recent analyses include CHEN Gang, *China's Climate Policy* (Routledge, 2012), Judith Shapiro, *China's Environmental Challenges* (2nd ed., Polity, 2016), Sophia Kalantzakos, *The EU, US and China Tackling Climate Change: Policies and Alliances for the Anthropocene* (Routledge, 2017), and David Sandalow, *Guide to Chinese Climate Policy 2018* (http://energypolicy.columbia.edu/sites/default/files/pictures/Guide%20to%20Chinese%20Climate%20Policy%207-20-18.pdf).

The best analysis of China's shift to a "new normal" economic development model is by Fergus Green and Nicholas Stern in their 2015 policy brief, "China's 'New Normal': Structural Change, Better Growth, and Peak Emissions" (http://www.lse.ac.uk/GranthamInstitute/wp-content/uploads/2015/06/China_new_normal_web1.pdf).

Further Reading

Isabel Hilton and Oliver Kerr provide a thoughtful analysis of the impact of China's "new normal" on its climate diplomacy in "The Paris Agreement: China's 'New Normal' Role in International Climate Negotiations," *Climate Policy*, 17, no. 1: 48–58 (2016). Isabel Hilton also edits chinadialogue (www.chinadialogue.net), an excellent bilingual website dedicated to promoting a common understanding of China's urgent environmental challenges.

The China Coal Consumption Cap Plan and Policy Research Project website (http://coalcap.nrdc.cn/?type=2) features a series of reports (in Chinese and English) concerning China's coal use, as discussed in Chapter 2 (see also https://www.nrdc.org/sites/default/files/china-coal-consumption-cap.pdf). Among other things, the Project published detailed recommendations for capping coal consumption in China's 13th Five Year Plan (https://d2ouvy59p0dg6k.cloudfront.net/downloads/china_coal_consumption_cap_plan_and_research_report__recommendations_for_the_13fyp.pdf). In order to help readers keep up with China's rapidly changing energy policy landscape and emission trends, China Energy Portal offers free English translations of Chinese energy policy, news, and statistics (https://chinaenergyportal.org/en/). Jeff Tollefson examines the forces behind recent emission trends and what they signal for the future in "Can the World Kick Its Fossil-Fuel Addiction Fast Enough?" (*Nature*, 25 April 2018).

The New Solar System, a major report from Stanford University's Jeffrey Ball and Dan Reicher (Steyer-Taylor Center for Energy Policy and Finance, 2017), illustrates the key drivers and challenges of the skyrocketing solar industry in China, as discussed in Chapter 3. The report also recommends changes in US solar policy that would put solar power on a more economically sensible path toward environmentally significant growth. Joanna Lewis (https://blogs.commons.georgetown.edu/jil9) has published extensively on renewable energy and green innovation in China, including her book, *Green Innovation in China: China's Wind Power Industry and the Global Transition to a Low-Carbon Economy* (Columbia University Press, 2013). In *The Greening of Asia: The Business Case for Solving Asia's Environmental Emergency* (Columbia University Press, 2015), Mark Clifford provides a behind-the-scenes look at how companies in China and elsewhere in Asia are building businesses that will lessen the environmental impact of the region's extraordinary economic growth. The Regulatory Assistance Project (www.raponline.org) provides in-depth analysis and practical recommendations for China's power sector reform and renewable energy integration. Bloomberg New Energy Finance (www.bnef.com) conducts independent research and publishes long-term forecasts on clean energy, including an authoritative annual report on global trends in renewable energy investment (https://www.bnef.com/core/insights/18365).

A fascinating new book on the broader issues surrounding the global electric vehicle industry (as discussed in Chapter 4) is Daniel Sperling, *Three Revolutions: Steering Automated, Shared and Electric Vehicles to a Better Future* (Island Press, 2018). Chapter 8 of Sperling's book examines whether China will be able to harness its electric vehicles, automation, and shared mobility to sharply reduce its smothering air pollution and carbon emissions. In an article in *Vox*, David Roberts explains how China is driving down costs and scaling up the global market for electric buses: "China Made Solar Panels Cheap. Now It's Doing the Same for Electric Buses" (https://www.vox.com/energy-and-environment/2018/4/17/17239368/china-investment-solar-electric-buses-cost).

For an in-depth analysis of China's green finance efforts (discussed in Chapter 5), see Sean Gilbert and Lihuan Zhou, *The Knowns and Unknowns of*

China's Green Finance (New Climate Economy, 2017). Kelly Sims Gallagher and Qi Qi published a comprehensive study of the environmental impacts of China's foreign direct investment in *Policies Governing China's Overseas Development Finance: Implications for Climate Change* (Center for International Environment and Resource Policy, The Fletcher School, Tufts University, 2018). The Paulson Institute publishes comprehensive reports on a wide range of Chinese economic and environmental topics, with a special focus on green finance (http://www.paulsoninstitute.org). Finally, a paper by Ehtisham Ahmad, Isabella Neuweg, and Nicholas Stern examines how China's Belt and Road Initiative could help build a connected and sustainable world economy: "China, the World and the Next Decade: Better Growth, Better Climate" (Grantham Research Institute on Climate Change and the Environment and Centre for Climate Change Economics and Policy, London School of Economics and Political Science, 2018).

Notes

Introduction: China –The New Climate Torchbearer?

1 World Meteorological Organization, *Greenhouse Gas Bulletin*. October 30, 2017.
2 World Bank Group, "Rapid, Climate-Informed Development Needed to Keep Climate Change from Pushing More than 100 Million People into Poverty by 2030." World Bank. November 8, 2015.
3 World Health Organization, "Climate Change and Health Fact Sheet." February 1, 2018.
4 Mooney, Chris and Brady Dennis, "The Military Paid for a Study on Sea Level Rise. The Results Were Scary." *Washington Post*, April 25, 2018.
5 *Quadrennial Defense Review 2014*. US Department of Defense. 2014.
6 *China Daily*, "Full Text of Xi Jinping's Report at 19th CPC National Congress." Chinadaily.com.cn. November 4, 2017.

Chapter 1 China's Climate Diplomacy

1 Economy, Elizabeth C., "The Impact of International Regimes on Chinese Foreign Policy-Making: Broadening Perspectives and Policies ... But Only to a Point." In *The Making of Chinese Foreign and Security Policy in the Era of Reform, 1978–2000*, ed. David M. Lampton (Stanford, CA: Stanford University Press, 2001).

2 Hatch, Michael T., "Chinese Politics, Energy Policy, and the International Climate Change Negotiations." In *Global Warming and East Asia: The Domestic and International Politics of Climate Change*, ed. Paul G. Harris (London: Routledge, 2003).

3 Hatch, "Chinese Politics."

4 Economy, "The Impact of International Regimes."

5 Hatch, "Chinese Politics."

6 Hatch, "Chinese Politics."

7 Economy, Elizabeth C., "China's Environmental Diplomacy." In *China and the World: Chinese Foreign Policy Faces the New Millennium*, ed. Samuel S. Kim (Boulder, CO: Westview Press, 1998).

8 Hatch, "Chinese Politics."

9 Economy, "China's Environmental Diplomacy."

10 Zhang, Zhihong, "The Forces behind China's Climate Change Policy: Interests, Sovereignty and Prestige." In *Global Warming and East Asia: The Domestic and International Politics of Climate Change*, ed. Paul G. Harris (London: Routledge, 2003).

11 Economy, "China's Environmental Diplomacy."

12 Chayes, Abram, and Charlotte J. Kim, "China and

the United Nations Framework Convention on Climate Change." In *Energizing China: Reconciling Environmental Protection and Economic Growth*, ed. Michael B. McElroy, Chris P. Nielsen, and P. Lydon (Cambridge, MA: HUCE/Harvard University Press, 1998).

13 Chayes and Kim, "China and the United Nations Framework Convention on Climate Change."

14 Chayes and Kim, "China and the United Nations Framework Convention on Climate Change."

15 "China's Economy and the WTO: All Change." *The Economist*. December 10, 2011.

16 Bradsher, Keith, and David Barboza, "Pollution from Chinese Coal Casts a Global Shadow." *New York Times*. June 11, 2006.

17 Cohen, Aaron J., H. Ross Anderson, Bart Ostro, Kiran Dev Pandey, Michal Krzyzanowski, Nino Künzli, Kersten Gutschmidt, et al., "The Global Burden of Disease Due to Outdoor Air Pollution." *Journal of Toxicology and Environmental Health, Part A*, 68, nos. 13–14 (2005): 1301–7; Kan, Haidong, "Environment and Health in China: Challenges and Opportunities." *Environmental Health Perspectives*, 117, no. 12 (2009); doi:10.1289/ehp.0901615.

18 "China Issues First 'Green GDP' Report." 中外对话 chinadialogue. July 9, 2006.

19 Conrad, Björn, "China in Copenhagen: Reconciling the 'Beijing Climate Revolution' and the 'Copenhagen Climate Obstinacy'." *The China Quarterly* (2012): 435–55; doi:10.1017/S0305741012000458.

20 Copsey, Tan, "Briefing: the Copenhagen Accord." 中外对话 chinadialogue. December 24, 2009.

21 Pasternack, Alex, "Blaming China for Copenhagen Won't Help the Climate"; https://www.treehugger.com/corporate-responsibility/blaming-china-for-copenhagen-wont-help-the-climate.html.

22 Watts, Jonathan, "Copenhagen Summit: China's Quiet Satisfaction at Tough Tactics and Goalless Draw." *Guardian*. December 20, 2009.

23 Wang-Kaeding, Heidi, "What Does Xi Jinping's New Phrase 'Ecological Civilization' Mean?" *The Diplomat*. March 6, 2018; Parr, Ben, and Don Henry, "China Moves Towards Ecological Civilisation." Australian Institute of International Affairs. August 24, 2016.

24 Xinhua, "Beijing Air Pollution Reaches Dangerous Levels." *China Daily*. January 13, 2013; World Health Organization, *WHO Air Quality Guidelines for Particulate Matter, Ozone, Nitrogen Dioxide and Sulfur Dioxide: Global Update 2005*. 2006.

25 Berkeley Earth, "Killer Air: Berkeley Earth Publishes Study on Air Pollution in China." August 2015.

26 Tan, Monica, "Bad to Worse: Ranking 74 Chinese Cities by Air Pollution." Greenpeace East Asia. February 19, 2014.

27 Zhao, Tianyu, "The Third National Assessment Report on Climate Change Was Released." November 23, 2015. China Meteorological News Press.

28 National Development and Reform Commission, "The National Strategy for Climate Change

Adaptation." Grantham Research Institute on Climate Change and the Environment. 2013.

29 The World Bank, "Which Coastal Cities Are at Highest Risk of Damaging Floods? New Study Crunches the Numbers." August 19, 2013; Holder, Josh, Niko Kommenda, and Jonathan Watts, "The Three-Degree World: The Cities that Will Be Drowned by Global Warming." *Guardian.* November 3, 2017.

30 Lu, Mia, and Joanna Lewis, *China and US Case Studies: Preparing for Climate Change.* Georgetown Climate Center. August 2015.

31 Wang, Binbin, Yating Shen, and Yangyang Jin, "Measurement of Public Awareness of Climate Change in China: Based on a National Survey with 4,025 Samples." *Chinese Journal of Population Resources and Environment*, 15, no. 4 (2017): 285–91; doi:10.1080/10042857.2017.1418276.

32 Energy Foundation China, *Climate Change in the Chinese Mind Survey Report 2017.* November 8, 2017.

33 Wu, Wencong, "Pollution 'to Ease in Five to 10 Years.'" China Daily. November 6, 2013.

34 Denyer, Simon, "China Confronts the Pain of Kicking its Coal Addiction." *Washington Post.* October 28, 2015.

35 Huang, Echo, and Tripti Lahiri, "Xi Jinping to China: 'Any Harm We Inflict on Nature Will Eventually Return to Haunt Us.'" *Quartz.* October 18, 2017.

Chapter 2 Dethroning Old King Coal

1 Li, Shuo, and Lauri Myllyvirta, "Beijing Won't Meet WHO Air Pollution Standards Until 2030s." Greenpeace East Asia. April 11, 2013.

2 Carrington, Damian. "China's Coal Peak Hailed as Turning Point in Climate Change Battle." *Guardian.* July 25, 2016.

3 Li, Shuyu, Xue Yang, and Rongrong Li, "Forecasting China's Coal Power Installed Capacity: A Comparison of MGM, ARIMA, GM-ARIMA, and NMGM Models." *Sustainability*, 10, no. 2 (2018): 506; doi:10.3390/su10020506.

4 Huang, Echo, "China's Putting the Brakes on Coal for Heating Millions of Homes this Winter." *Quartz.* October 4, 2017; https://qz.com/1093898/chinas-putting-the-brakes-on-coal-for-heating-millions-of-homes-this-winter/.

5 "China's National Coal Cap Policy Could Save Nearly 50,000 Lives and $6.2 billion Every Year by 2020." Natural Resources Defense Council. April 8, 2015.

6 Chen, Yuyu, Avraham Ebenstein, Michael Greenstone, and Li Hongbin, "Evidence on the Impact of Sustained Exposure to Air Pollution on Life Expectancy from China's Huai River Policy." *Proceedings of the National Academy of Sciences*, 2013.

7 International Energy Agency, *Energy Efficiency Market Report 2016.* October 2016.

8 Hart, Melanie, Luke Bassett, and Blaine Johnson, "Everything You Think You Know About Coal in

China Is Wrong." Center for American Progress. May 15, 2017.

9 Hart, et al., "Everything You Think You Know About Coal in China Is Wrong."

10 Nie, Winter, "Here's Why China Laying Off 1.8 Million Workers Is Actually Good News." *Fortune*. March 4, 2016.

11 Feng, Coco, and Dong Jing, "Big Coal Burning Less Money, but Remains Buried in Debt." *Caixin Global*. July 19, 2017; https://www.caixinglobal.com/2017-07-19/101118846.html.

12 International Renewable Energy Agency, *Renewable Energy and Jobs – Annual Review 2017*. 2017.

13 Forsythe, Michael, "China Aims to Spend at Least $360 Billion on Renewable Energy by 2020." *New York Times*. January 5, 2017.

14 Natural Resources Defense Council, "China's Coal Cap Policy Will Increase Country's Clean Energy Jobs." March 26, 2015.

15 Molinaroli, Alex, "China's Clean, Green Buildings of the Future." World Economic Forum. June 21, 2017; https://www.weforum.org/agenda/2017/06/china-clean-green-buildings-future/.

16 Spencer, Thomas, Nicolas Berghmans, and Oliver Sartor, *Coal Transitions in China's Power Sector: A Plant-Level Assessment of Stranded Assets and Retirement Pathways*. IDDRI. November 2017.

17 Boren, Zachary Davies, "China Suspends Permits for New Coal Plants as Overcapacity Policy Bites." *Unearthed*. May 16, 2017.

18 Daley, Jason, "China Turns on the World's Largest Floating Solar Farm." Smithsonian.com. June 7, 2017; https://www.smithsonianmag.com/smart‑news/china‑launches‑largest‑floating‑solar‑farm‑180963587/.

19 Greenpeace, *Estimating Carbon Emissions from China's Coal-to-Chemical Industry during the "13th Five-year Plan" Period*. 2017.

20 Reuters, "Chinese Truck Makers Fined US$5.8m for Emissions Fraud and Breaching Pollution Standards." *South China Morning Post*. January 9, 2018.

21 The Institute of Public & Environmental Affairs, "IPE's Mission: Promoting Information Disclosure and Advancing Multi-Party Participation, to Bring Back Blue Skies and Clear Waters"; http://wwwen.ipe.org.cn/about/about.aspx.

22 International Energy Agency, "Medium-Term Coal Market Report 2016." December 2016.

23 Myllyvirta, Lauri, "Air Pollution: Beijing Starts the Biggest Shut Down of Steel Factories in History." *Unearthed*. October 30, 2017.

24 Yicai Global, "中国改善空气质量的"模式"出来了：环保部专家概括为20个字 [China's Air Quality Improvement Model Released: Ministry of Environmental Protection Experts Summarize in 20 Words]." February 2, 2018.

25 Xu, Muyu, and David Stanway. "Beijing Meets 2017 Air Pollution Target Set Under 2013 Clean-Up Plan." Reuters. January 3, 2018.

Chapter 3 Catalyzing the Clean Energy Revolution

1 Biello, David, "Where Did the Carter White House's Solar Panels Go?" *Scientific American.* August 6, 2010.
2 Personal communication with the author, February 2018.
3 Higgins, Andrew, "With Solar Valley Project, China Embarks on Bold Green Technology Mission." *Washington Post.* May 17, 2010.
4 Jervey, Ben, "China Is Showing the World What Renewable Energy Dominance Looks Like." *Ecowatch.* October 4, 2017; Bradford, Abi, Gideon Weissman, Rob Sargent, and Bret Fanshaw, "Shining Cities 2017: How Smart Local Policies Are Expanding Solar Power in America." Frontier Group and Environment America Research & Policy Center. 2017.
5 National Development and Reform Commission, *China: 12th Five-Year Plan of Renewable Energy Development*, trans. Wiley Rein LLP. Policy Brief. 2012.
6 Global Wind Energy Council, and International Renewable Energy Agency, *30 Years of Policies for Wind Energy: Lessons from China.* July 22, 2013.
7 Institute for Energy Economics & Financial Analysis, *IEEFA Report: China in 2017 Continued to Position Itself for Global Clean Energy Dominance.* January 9, 2018.
8 Gardiner, Beth, "Three Reasons to Believe in China's Renewable Energy Boom." *National Geographic.* May 12, 2017.

9 Jing, Yan, and Lauri Myllyvirta, "China Has Already Surpassed Its 2020 Solar Target." *Unearthed*. August 24, 2017.

10 International Energy Agency, "Renewables 2017: Analysis and Forecasts to 2022." October 4, 2017; https://www.iea.org/publications/renewables2017/.

11 Global Wind Energy Council, and International Renewable Energy Agency, *30 Years of Policies for Wind Energy*.

12 Global Wind Energy Council, "Wind in Numbers"; http://gwec.net/global-figures/wind-in-numbers/.

13 GlobalData, "China's Wind Power Installed Capacity Will Escalate to 495 GW by 2030, says GlobalData." May 5, 2016.

14 Colville, Finlay, "Top 10 Module Suppliers in 2017." *PV Tech*. January 15, 2018.

15 Osborne, Mark, "Planned Solar Manufacturing Capacity Expansions Bigger than Expected in 1H 2017." *PV Tech*. October 9, 2017.

16 Jaffe, Amy Myers, "Green Giant: Renewable Energy and Chinese Power." *Foreign Affairs*. February 16, 2018.

17 National Renewable Energy Laboratory, "Solar Photovoltaic Manufacturing Cost Analysis." September 5, 2013.

18 Jiang, Kejun, and Jonathan Woetzel, "China's Renewable-Energy Revolution." Project Syndicate. August 21, 2017; https://www.project-syndicate.org/commentary/china-renewable-energy-revolution-by-jiang-kejun-and-jonathan-woetzel-2017-08?barrier=accesspaylog.

19 Bloomberg New Energy Finance. "Global Trends in Renewable Energy Investment Report 2018." April 5, 2018; http://fs-unep-centre.org/publications/global-trends-renewable-energy-investment-report-2018.

20 Ball, Jeffrey, Dan Reicher, Xiaojing Sun, and Caitlin Pollock, "The New Solar System." Steyer-Taylor Center for Energy Policy and Finance. March 21, 2017.

21 International Energy Agency, "Renewables 2017."

22 Bloomberg New Energy Finance, "Global Trends in Renewable Energy Investment Report 2018."

23 International Energy Agency, "Renewables 2017."

24 Bloomberg New Energy Finance, "New Energy Outlook 2017." June 21, 2017.

25 Needleman, David Berney, Jeremy R. Poindexter, Rachel C. Kurchin, I. Marius Peters, Gregory Wilson, and Tonio Buonassisi, "Economically Sustainable Scaling of Photovoltaics to Meet Climate Targets." IEEE 43rd Photovoltaic Specialists Conference (PVSC), 2016; doi:10.1109/pvsc.2016.7750316.

26 Ball et al., "The New Solar System."

27 "2017 US Energy and Employment Report." Department of Energy. 2017.

28 Ettenson, Lara, "US Clean Energy Jobs Surpass Fossil Fuel Employment." Natural Resources Defense Council. February 8, 2017.

29 Ettenson, "US Clean Energy Jobs Surpass Fossil Fuel Employment."

30 "Fastest Growing Occupations: Occupational Outlook Handbook." US Bureau of Labor Statistics. April 13, 2018.

31 Ryan, David, "The Effects of Section 201 Safeguards on US Industries." *Georgetown Journal of International Law*, 44 (2012).

32 Ball et al., "The New Solar System."

33 Davidson, M. R., "Creating Markets for Wind Electricity in China: Case Studies in Energy Policy and Regulation." PhD thesis. Massachusetts Institute of Technology, 2018.

34 "China's Embrace of a New Electricity-Transmission Technology Holds Lessons for Others." *The Economist*. January 14, 2017.

35 Li, Ying. "Blowing in the Wind." 中外对话 chinadialogue. May 31, 2016.

36 Bloomberg News, "China Is Adding Solar Power at a Record Pace." July 19, 2017; https://www.bloomberg.com/news/articles/2017-07-19/china-adds-about-24gw-of-solar-capacity-in-first-half-official.

37 "US–China Joint Presidential Statement on Climate Change." National Archives and Records Administration. September 25, 2015.

38 EVAdoption, "EVs as Demand Response Vehicles for the Power Grid and Excess Clean Energy." February 18, 2018; http://evadoption.com/evs-as-demand-response-vehicles-for-the-power-grid-and-excess-clean-energy/.

Chapter 4 *Jumpstarting the Electric Vehicle Industry*

1 Zhou, Oceana, "CNPC Forecasts Chinese 2018 Oil Demand to Grow 5% to 12 Million B/d." S&P Global. January 16, 2018; https://www.platts.com/

latest - news / oil / singapore / cnpc - forecasts - chinese - 2018-oil-demand-to-grow-27906041. US Energy Information Administration, FAQ, "How Much Oil Consumed by the United States Comes from Foreign Countries?" EIA Energy Conference. April 4, 2018.

2 Friedman, Thomas L., "Their Moon Shot and Ours." *New York Times*. September 25, 2010.

3 De Neve, Pinar Akcayoz, "Electric Vehicles in China." Policy Brief. Belfer Center, Harvard Kennedy School. June 2014.

4 "California: ZEV." Transport Policy; https://www. transportpolicy.net/standard/california-zev/.

5 Clover, Charles, "Electric Cars: China's Highly Charged Power Play." *Financial Times*. October 12, 2017.

6 Bloomberg News. "China Plans to Kill Local Subsidies for Electric Cars." December 17, 2017; https://www. bloomberg.com/news/articles/2017-12-18/china-is-said-to-plan-killing-local-subsidies-for-electric-cars-jbbq58bn.

7 Meng, Jing, "China's Largest Ride-Hailing Firm Wants to Rent You an Electric Car." *South China Morning Post*. December 5, 2017.

8 Clover, "Electric Cars."

9 Cui, Hongyang, *China's New Energy Vehicle Mandate Policy (Final Rule)*. The International Council on Clean Transportation. January 11, 2018.

10 Clover, Charles, "China's Electric Car Push Set to Trigger 'War of Attrition'." *Financial Times*. November 14, 2017.

11 Lambert, Fred, "Virtually All Automakers (except for

Tesla) Are Currently Lobbying to Block EPA's New Fuel Consumption Standard." *Electrek*. December 9, 2016.

12 Hove, Anders, "These Four Lessons Will Help China Win the Electric Vehicle Market." 中外对话 china-dialogue. September 5, 2017.

13 Jeremy Hodges, "China's Bus Electrification Proceeds at Full Gallop." Bloomberg. April 25, 2018.

14 "China Plug-in Sales for 2017-Q4 and Full Year – Update." EV-Volumes – The Electric Vehicle World Sales Database.

15 Bateman, Joshua. "The Biggest Electric Vehicle Company You've Never Heard Of." Fast Company. January 22, 2018; BYD Motors Inc., "BYD Unveils North America's Largest Electric Bus Factory with Bipartisan Group of Senior Officials." *Mass Transit*. October 16, 2017.

16 Turrentine, Jeff, "Could Peak Oil Demand Be Just a Dozen Years Away?" Natural Resources Defense Council. January 26, 2018.

17 Ryan, Joe, "China Is About to Bury Elon Musk in Batteries." June 28, 2017; https://www.bloomberg.com/news/articles/2017-06-28/china-is-about-to-bury-elon-musk-in-batteries.

18 Shane, Daniel, "China Is Winning 'Arms Race' For Electric Cars." CNNMoney.

19 Perkowski, Jack, "EV Batteries: A $240 Billion Industry in the Making that China Wants to Take Charge Of." *Forbes*. August 3, 2017.

20 Ma, Jie, David Stringer, Yan Zhang, and Sohee Kim, "The Breakneck Rise of China's Colossus of

Electric-Car Batteries." February 1, 2018; https://www.bloomberg.com/news/features/2018-02-01/the-breakneck-rise-of-china-s-colossus-of-electric-car-batteries.

21 Natural Resources Defense Council, the Energy Research Institute of the National Development and Reform Commission, and the Energy Storage Alliance, 电动汽车储能技术潜力及经济性研究. [The Economics and Application Potential of Electric Vehicles in Energy Storage Technologies]. February 2018.

22 Hannon, Eric, Colin McKerracher, Itamar Orlandi, and Surya Ramkumar, *An Integrated Perspective on the Future of Mobility*. McKinsey & Company. October 2016.

23 Bloomberg New Energy Finance, "Electric Vehicle Outlook 2017." July, 2017.

24 Liu, Jian, Hyoungmi Kim, and Tang Li, *The Potential of Grid Integration of Electric Vehicles in Shanghai*. Natural Resources Defense Council. October 2016.

25 Battaglia, Sarah, "The Newest Demand Response Participant: Electric Vehicles." *The Energy Collective*. November 3, 2014.

26 Natural Resources Defense Council et al., 电动汽车储能技术潜力及经济性研究.

27 Moss, Trefor, "China, with Methodical Discipline, Conjures a Market for Electric Cars." *Wall Street Journal*. October 2, 2017.

Chapter 5 Greening China's Financial System

1 People's Bank of China, et al., "Dr. Ma Jun." Climate Finance Day. 2016.

2 Finamore, Barbara, and Yan Wang, "China's Focus on Green Finance at the G20 and Beyond." Natural Resources Defense Council. December 15, 2016.

3 Climate Bonds Initiative and the China Central Depository & Clearing Company, *China Green Bond Market 2016*. January 2017.

4 Darby, Megan, "China is Taking the Green Bond Market by Storm." *Climate Home News*. January 16, 2017.

5 Han, Xue, "Ma Jun: Europe and China Have Different Priorities on Green Finance." 中外对话 chinadialogue. October 24, 2017

6 Climate Bonds Initiative and China Central Depository & Clearing Company. *China Green Bond Market 2017*. February 2018.

7 G20 Green Finance Study Group, *G20 Green Finance Synthesis Report*. 2017.

8 UN Environment Programme, "G20 Leaders Welcome 'Green Finance' in Summit Communiqué." News release. September 5, 2016; http://unepinquiry.org/news/g20-leaders-welcome-green-finance-in-summit-communique/.

9 Chen, Han, "US–China Peer Review – Billions in Fossil Fuel Subsidies." Natural Resources Defense Council. September 19, 2016.

10 Chen, Han, and Noah Lerner, "G20 Countries' Public Coal Financing Reaches Five-Year High."

Natural Resources Defense Council. February 8, 2018.

11 UN Environment Programme, "UN Environment Appoints Sustainable Finance Guru Dr. Ma Jun as Special Advisor." News release. September 8, 2017.

12 Caldecott, Ben, "A Green BRI Is a Global Imperative." 中外对话 chinadialogue. December 15, 2017.

13 Gamio, Lazaro, and Erica Pandey, "The Staggering Scale of China's Belt and Road initiative." *Axios*. January 19, 2018.

14 China Global Green Leadership. "Green Development under Belt and Road Initiative: Pushing Forward the Global Implementation of the Paris Agreement"; http://www.chinagoinggreen.org/en/?p=6951.

15 Gallagher, Kevin, "China Global Energy Finance: A New Interactive Database." Global Economic Governance Initiative Policy Brief 002, March 2017.

16 Peng, Ren, et al. "China's Involvement in Coal-Fired Power Projects along the Belt and Road." Global Environmental Institute. May 2017.

17 Darby, Megan, "Belt and Road Countries Could Emit Triple China's Carbon, Warns Official." *Climate Home News*. December 11, 2017.

18 "Full Text of President Xi's Speech at Opening of Belt and Road Forum." Xinhua. May 14, 2017.

19 "Joint Communique of the Leaders Roundtable of the Belt and Road Forum for International Cooperation." May 16, 2017; http://www.beltandroadforum.org/english/n100/2017/0516/c22-423.html.

20 *Guidance on Promoting Green Belt and Road.* Belt and Road Portal. May 8, 2017; https://eng.yidaiyilu. gov.cn/zchj/qwfb/12479.htm.

21 Zhang, Chun, and Yao Zhe, "China on Path to Greener Foreign Investment." chinadialogue. October 3, 2017.

22 Buckley, Tim, Simon Nicholas, and Melissa Brown, *China 2017 Review: World's Second-Biggest Economy Continues to Drive Global Trends in Energy Investment.* Institute for Energy Economics and Financial Analysis. January 2018.

23 Chen, Han, "G20 Countries' Public Coal Financing Reaches Five-Year High." Natural Resources Defense Council. February 9, 2018.

24 Buckley et al., *China 2017 Review.*

25 Chen, "G20 Countries' Public Coal Financing Reaches Five-Year High."

26 *The Way Forward: Five Key Actions to Achieving a Low Energy Sector.* International Energy Agency. 2014.

27 "China Responsible for Over Half of Global Energy Conservation: Climate Chief." *Global Times – Xinhua.* November 20, 2015.

28 Kallakuri, Chetana, Shruti Vaidyanathan, Meegan Kelly, and Rachel Cluett, *The 2016 International Energy Efficiency Scorecard.* American Council for an Energy-Efficient Economy. July 2016.

29 Carter, Sheryl, "Efficiency Gains Globally, Two-Thirds of Savings Untapped." Natural Resources Defense Council. October 25, 2016.

30 International Energy Agency, "Renewables 2017:

Analysis and Forecasts to 2022." October, 2017; https://www.iea.org/publications/renewables2017/.

31 International Finance Corporation, "IFC Study Finds Climate Pact Helped Open Up $23 Trillion in Emerging-Market Opportunities." News release. November 7, 2016; https://ifcext.ifc.org/ifcext/Press room/IFCPressRoom.nsf/0/BDD8E660E454DDD78 5258064004B4814.

Epilogue

1 Ball, Jeffrey, Dan Reicher, Xiaojing Sun, and Caitlin Pollock, "The New Solar System." Steyer-Taylor Center for Energy Policy and Finance. March 21, 2017.